# Writing My Life

## A Patchwork of Memories

Terry C. Ley

*Writing My Life* is a memoir,
a collection of life stories from the author's life in Iowa and Alabama..

Copyright © 2018 Terry C. Ley

ISBN-13: 978-1730719288

Ley, Terry C.

Writing My Life/ by Terry C. Ley

Cover Illustration "Patchwork Man" by James OBrien

Cover and Layout Design by Bob Hranichny

# Contents

# Dedication

*For those who have shaped and added texture to my patchwork quilt life..*

*my parents...*

*my teachers...*

*my students...*

*my friends and relatives...*

*my readers...*

*Mari, my kindest critic*

# *Writes of Passage*

**M**uch of the writing that I have done as an adult I have done under duress. As an undergraduate and graduate college student in English and education, I met frequent deadlines by grinding out papers requiring literary analysis or pedagogical insight. As a high school teacher I wrote curriculum guides during summers, sandwiching that writing between obligations to produce graduate papers and, finally, my dissertation. At thirty-five I volunteered for a "publish or perish" career at Auburn University, where my employers measured my worth (in part) by the number of articles I published in national professional journals. Those pieces were most valuable—to the University and to me—if they reported research that I had undertaken. During the twenty-seven years that I walked under that cloud, writing often became something of a demon. Would I publish—or perish? My fate lay in the hands of editors of academic journals, whom I would never meet.

Earlier in my life, in Iowa, I had viewed writing not as a threatening cloud but as an opportunity to express myself, to

1

communicate to others ideas of some importance to me. In 1950, the *Cedar Falls Daily Record* published my Fire Prevention Week essay, a simple piece for which I won a certificate (on which my last name was misspelled) and some limited local acclaim. Letters to my grandmother, my aunts, and my English pen pal were rewarded with their responses in the return mail. An obedient student, I wrote what my teachers assigned without complaint, often gaining personal satisfaction from what I wrote. Usually, my teachers rewarded my writing with high marks, which nurtured my desire to write well, to please or somehow satisfy my limited real audience. Unfortunately, my teachers—and my faithful, supportive mother—were usually my only audiences for those school pieces. My teachers rarely posted, praised, or shared our writing with classmates.

Writing became more satisfying to me when I was in the ninth grade and our junior high school principal invited me to become editor of a new weekly school page in the *Cedar Falls Daily Record*. I accepted his invitation with enthusiasm, thus beginning a period of eight years as a school journalist, writing news articles, columns, and editorials that my peers, their parents, my teachers, and other members of my hometown and college communities read and often responded to. My journalistic experiences taught me to choose my topics and my words with care, made me acutely aware that my audiences were diverse, often appreciative, sometimes critical. Having responsive audiences energized me as a writer and made me more confident whenever I faced a blank sheet of paper.

When I retired in 2001, I was glad to leave the publish-or-perish cloud behind me. I looked forward to reading what I wanted to read and writing what I wanted to write—when I chose to read or write at all. I joined the Osher Lifelong Learning Institute at Auburn University (OLLI at Auburn) the following fall with great anticipation because I wanted to continue to learn after leaving an academic work setting. One of the first courses that I took was devoted to reading essays by Alabama writers who focused on how their lives in Alabama had influenced their writing. During our discussions, classmates seemed anxious to share their own stories. I saw a need for a course that would encourage seasoned adults to write their own life stories, and Writing Our Lives was born. What I planned as a single nine-week course has continued for fifteen years, three terms each year. We read published memoirs, we write our own life stories, and, when we're ready, we share them orally and in printed form with each other. We remember, we write, we share, we laugh, we weep, we write again.

In *Saving Our Lives* Richard L. Morgan wrote, "Our lives are like a patchwork quilt, and it is only in the evening of life that we can see the pattern of what we have woven. That is your payoff, your great reward for recollecting and saving your story." Writing Our Lives has given me an abundance of opportunities to explore those patterns in my life and has encouraged me to write about episodes that reflect those themes and to share what I write with an appreciative and responsive audience of peers. Writing has once again become a personal, reflective process with tangible rewards that are both liberating and satisfying.

What I have gathered here are some squares from my patchwork quilt to share with you.

# My Journey with Nicodemus

An only child, I longed for pets, but, because we lived in an apartment, my parents resisted allowing me to have a pet until I was six. And then, because puppies made too much noise and required too much care, I was permitted to have a turtle. Although I suppose I was disappointed not to be able to have the cocker spaniel of my dreams, I remember taking great care to choose just the right turtle at Woolworth's, the only store in our small Iowa town that offered them for sale. How does one choose a turtle? The fastest one? The biggest one? The friendliest one? I do not recall my criteria for judging which turtle was the best one for me, but I do remember carrying him home in a small cardboard box and introducing him to the small aquarium bowl, also purchased at Woolworth's, where he would live. What a splendid day it was, that day when I first had a living creature to play with and to care for!

Living creatures must, of course, have names—and in naming this turtle I outdid myself. First, because I was not highly aware of gender at six, I assumed that the turtle was a boy, like me. Next, I gave him a series of names, to see which one fit him best. I did not confer names on him at random, however. I was an avid reader—and what I couldn't read, my mother read to me—and the books that I loved became sources for naming my turtle. That turtle had a series of identities during the first few months of his residence in our apartment, depending upon whether my mother and I were reading from my Raggedy Ann and Raggedy Andy books, the latest installment by Uncle Wiggly in our newspaper, or any of the many books that we borrowed from the library. After I changed his name several times, my mother cautioned me that having so many names might confuse the turtle—or, worse, make him sick. Never wishing harm upon anyone—and surely not wishing to create either confusion or illness in this dear creature in my care—I ceased the renaming process and settled on calling my turtle Nicodemus, a name whose source I cannot now recall.

While it had been easy for me to imagine playing with a puppy, maybe even a kitten, I was challenged to find ways to amuse both Nicodemus and me. I talked to him a good bit, but he was not a conversationalist. He ate, of course, and I enjoyed watching him snap to retrieve the food that I sprinkled in his bowl. I also enjoyed taking Nicodemus for walks in our apartment. On our walks he took his time, to enjoy the scenery, I guessed; an impatient tour guide, I nudged him from behind, urging him to move those little legs faster and faster. One of our routine excursions together on Sunday afternoons was to visit my snoozing father in the living room. On those journeys we trudged past familiar landmarks—the monolithic wooden stepstool by the kitchen door, then, like giant Sequoias, the mahogany legs of the dining room table and chairs, through the oppressive heat emanating from the floor vent, and, finally, across the carpet-desert in the living room. Our destination was the davenport, on which lay my father, eyes closed, mouth open, newspaper resting on his chest. After airlifting Nicodemus to the giant's arm, I watched him begin his slow ascent toward the cave of the giant's mouth. On the best visits, Dad somehow sensed our presence and awoke, feigned surprise, and shooed us back toward Nicodemus's home in the kitchen before resuming his restful position.

Again, Mom warned me that I might be endangering Nicodemus by insisting on such arduous journeys, and, although I took her warning under advisement, I persisted in taking him for long walks.

Sure enough, one Monday morning, after such an expedition, when I went to feed Nicodemus, he seemed to be asleep, lounging on his rock as he did many hours each day. But he did not move when I sprinkled the tempting grainy morsels before him. He did not move when I nudged him, first gently, then with some vigor. Finally, even after I pushed him into the water, he did not move.

Nicodemus was dead, quite dead—and worse than my awareness of his deadness and my sense of loss was my realization that I had probably caused his death by changing his name so often and insisting on his frequent journeys to the far reaches of his world. After trying to assure me that I had not caused Nicodemus to die, my mother helped me to decide what to do with Nicodemus. Because no one close to me had died, I had only a rudimentary understanding of what it means to die. The books that I read were happy books in which no one died. I had seen few movies, but I surely enjoyed the cartoons that I saw at the Regent Theater when my Grandma Ley took me there—and in those cartoons, of course, mortally injured mice kept coming back to life. In Sunday school, I had learned about Jesus. He had died. But, like those mice, he too came back to life. Nicodemus didn't look like he was coming back to life any time soon. The one thing I knew about death was that, when people die, they were put in boxes and buried. I needed to bury Nicodemus, I told my mother. She helped me find an old cigar box and line it with toilet paper. Using a tablespoon, Mom lifted Nicodemus from his aquarium and laid him in the cigar box. I grabbed the cigar box and the tablespoon and headed out the kitchen door and down the steps toward Nicodemus's final resting place.

I knew that people had funerals at churches before they went to the cemetery, although I had never been to a funeral. Fortunately, St. Luke's Episcopal Church was at the end of our block, and that's where I headed. I might have preferred a Presbyterian burial because we were Presbyterians, but our church was two blocks away, and because I was not allowed to cross the busy streets yet by myself, I settled for an Episcopalian burial for dear, dead Nicodemus.

Next to the church wall, under some tall shrubs, I measured out the black dirt, spoonful by spoonful, until the hole was deep enough to conceal Nicodemus' tiny coffin. Before covering the box again, I checked inside, just in case Nicodemus had been resurrected during his journey to the Episcopal church. Nope, still quite dead. I turned my grieving self toward home.

Several days later, Nicodemus was still on my mind, and I began to wonder what would happen if he came back to life and found himself in that box. That would be pretty scary. I decided to check on him. After hastening to the burial site, bearing no tool or weapon, down on my haunches, I carefully brushed off the layer of dirt that covered the cigar box and lifted it out of the hole very carefully. What would I find inside? Nicodemus, deader than a doornail? Nicodemus, alive, alert, ready for another journey? When I lifted the lid, to solve that mystery, I was faced with another mystery, this one even scarier: *the box was empty*! No Nicodemus at all, not dead, not alive. Again, I thought of Jesus. Maybe Nicodemus had come back to life, gotten out of the box, and lumbered away. If he had, he had probably wandered across Seventh Street, to Jack DeBlauwe's yard. I pitied Nicodemus if he had fallen into the hands of Jack DeBlauwe because Jack was a bully who often threw rocks at my friends and me when he saw us in the alley. Surely Jack had it in him to be a grave robber, too.

To explore Jack's turf meant that I would have to cross the street, though, which meant that it was forbidden territory for me. I weighed the alternatives: having Mom angry with me for crossing the street (if she found out!) or rescuing Nicodemus from the clutches of the demon Jack. So, I compromised. I looked both ways (which would have pleased my mother) and crossed the street into enemy territory. Once there, I walked up Seventh Street to Main Street, then turned down Main Street, searching for signs of my turtle as I walked. Past Jack's house (where there were no signs of illicit activity) I walked, past the Whites' house (nothing there), to the First Christian Church, where I sat down on the low wall that separated the church's property from the sidewalk. Movement below drew my eyes to the gnarled roots of an old tree on the church side of the wall. There I saw a legion of giant black ants surrounding the ruined remains of my Nicodemus. My first reaction was shock, then fear, then sadness, then wonder. Was this what happened to animals after they died? And to people, too? My second reaction was to return Nicodemus where he belonged. I remember being shaken as I picked his corpse up and put it in the box, then hurried back up Main Street, across Seventh Street, and under the shrubs at the Episcopal church, where I reburied my turtle.

Although I still think that Jack DeBlauwe was the culprit who took Nicodemus from his cigar box and abandoned him at the First Christian Church, I cannot be sure. Nor can I be certain what led me to discover his ruined body or to return it to the grave that I had prepared. Regardless, I am confident that my turtle's demise helped prepare me to deal later with death, guilt, loss, and the transience of life.

# A Kindergarten Possum

If she were here today, my mother would tell you that I fought sleep when I was a child. I longed to stay up late and rise early. I disliked naps immensely. So, often I just pretended to sleep, to satisfy my mother. I'm sure she was wise to my playing possum, closing my eyes, feigning sleep, when she entered my bedroom to check on me. Sometimes she bribed me to get me to take an afternoon nap. "After you wake up, we'll go to Roger's house," she would promise. Roger was my best friend—and Roger's mother was my mother's best friend—so I guess we were both anxious for naptime to end on those occasions.

Perhaps then it will not surprise you to learn that there were only two things I didn't like about Miss McGrane's kindergarten class: that I got to go to school only during the mornings and that, smack dab in the middle of each and every morning, we wasted valuable time by taking naps!

When naptime came, I dawdled until the very last possible moment, finally lying down on my little purple rug, transformed, now a possum in kindergarten. Once reasonably comfortable, I obediently closed my eyes, but I kept my ears wide open. While others napped, I heard the loud-ticking classroom clock, the big hand marking each torturous minute with a giant leap forward; footsteps of lucky first-grade children, who stayed at school all day and took no naps, on their way to the bathrooms; the restless sounds of classmates shifting positions on their own rugs; and, occasionally, the quiet voice of Miss McGrane, reminding someone not so good at playing possum to settle down and close his eyes.

The best sounds on those mornings, though, were Miss McGrane's footsteps, when she tiptoed across the floor at the end of our naptime, stepping around little children on their little rugs on her way to our piano in the corner. Having reached her destination, she carefully slid the stool out, sat down on it, and played a quiet wake-up song to end our naptime, a melody chosen from her impressive repertoire of kindergarten crowd-pleasers.

I daresay no one in the room was happier to hear that melody every school day morning than the possum on the purple rug who, transformed by his teacher's music, became again a red-haired boy anxious to go about his kindergarten business.

# *Home on East Street*

**M**y childhood home had several lives before my father made it my childhood home. Before Dad bought it in 1947, the shell of our house had served as a country church and as a general store. During and immediately after World War II, new home construction was forbidden, but one could remodel or renovate existing structures. Dad bought the building ("cash on the barrelhead," his motto) with his share of the sale of his family's apartment house on Main Street, moved the building to East Street, and committed nearly all of his "spare time" for the rest of his life to perfecting it for our lives together.

Dad took me to see the shell of our new home before he had it moved. It sat ugly and forlorn, on cement blocks, in the middle of an overgrown lot on College Hill in our hometown, having been moved there from a rural site somewhere else in the county. Although several of its windows were broken, there was a padlock on the door that Dad worked on while I stood beside him, anxious for a first peek inside. Stepping across the threshold, I saw only what Dad's flashlight revealed:

one undivided space, not very large, it seemed to me, dark and spooky. Some of the plaster had cracked and fallen to the floor during the moving process. The warped floorboards creaked as I stepped further inside, stirring up dust with every step.

When Dad asked, "What do you think?" as he often did when we were considering anything together, I said I thought it looked much smaller than our apartment.

"This will be just our kitchen and living room," he said. "The rest will come later."

What he didn't mention then was that we would live in the basement under this building while he prepared the kitchen and living room above us. Later, I watched with wonder the team of horses digging the basement; I watched impatiently while Dad laid each cement block that formed the foundation, wishing that the house could spring up overnight, knowing that it could not.

We were able to remain in our apartment until the basement was ready for us. Mom's life at home probably changed little during that time. A continuing cycle of cleaning, cooking, washing, and ironing seemed to satisfy her then. I attended third grade each day, then returned home to play with neighborhood friends until suppertime. Dad's life became much more complicated, however: rising at 5:00 a.m., unloading trucks at John Deere's from 7:00 to 4:00, then working on East Street until after dark on weekdays and all day on most Saturdays and Sundays. On those occasions when he invited me to go to East Street with him, I sometimes helped him by holding wood while he measured carefully and sawed precisely; at other times, I played with new friends who lived in the neighborhood, often in the open field next door to our new house. Too often, I was ready to leave the worksite and return to our apartment long before Dad was ready to call it a day.

Life in our basement was decidedly cozy. In the kitchen at the north end, near the steps, were the familiar appliances we had moved from our apartment, joined by my mother's Maytag wringer washing machine. Three clotheslines ran the length of the room, ready for service on rainy Mondays. Never one to waste space, Dad had built a large pantry under the basement steps. At the other end of the room, next to the fuel oil tank, were my parents' bed and dresser. At the foot of their bed was the toilet, partially surrounded by the cardboard casing that had encircled the new water heater, that makeshift screen our only hope for privacy. Between the bottom of the basement steps and the toilet was our daybed, which served as davenport by day, as my bed at night. A small window at each end of the room admitted precious little light; however, the north window allowed us to view the ankles of anyone who approached the back door. Although we had moved from a reasonably commodious and comfortable apartment to this cramped living space, I do not remember resenting the move or the inconveniences with which we all dealt. I suspect that my mother's memories of this place were darker than mine, for she remained there alone all day, nearly every day, without easy transportation. Undoubtedly all of us often yearned for privacy not readily available whenever we were "at home."

How happy we must have been when we moved most of our possessions upstairs two years later. Our old refrigerator and stove made that move, of course, but my parents' bed remained in the basement, now our guest room. In the living room Dad built in a Murphy in-a-door bed for Mom and him, surely a novelty to all of us because, at night, when Mom opened the French doors and pulled it down, the bed nearly filled the center of the living room. I slept in a real bed again, a rollaway bed that lived in the kitchen pantry throughout the day, between the stove and the kitchen table at night. I kept my precious toys and books in newly available spaces in the basement, where I also once again enjoyed quiet privacy for indoor play—until someone needed to use the toilet, still located behind the water-heater-packing-case screen in the basement.

By that time, Dad could get a permit to add to the house, and he began the second phase of his project that became the two bedrooms and a bathroom completing our family home. He continued to work on the house for several hours each weeknight, most Saturdays, Sundays, and vacations. I was old enough by then to observe the care with which my father completed each task: mixing cement, measuring twice and cutting once, applying paint with the grain. Occasionally he invited me to help him, often using those times to teach me how to apply cement, to measure accurately, to use saws responsibly, to cover surfaces with paint without streaking or dribbling. I must have shown little talent for those tasks—and, frankly, not a whole lot of interest—but I remember only his patience whenever I attempted to help him build our house.

About two years later, we moved into the new addition. What joy I felt, to have my own bedroom again at last, my own closet, a place for my desk, my books! What joy, to use a bathroom with a door on it, to be able to take a bath again instead of always taking a shower!

Although our house was then complete in one sense—we were living in its five rooms—Dad never finished improving and refining it. He landscaped the property. He built a garage one summer. He remodeled the kitchen to accommodate my mother's new refrigerator. He built a maple cupboard for my record collection in my bedroom. Indeed, the house remained a work in progress until Dad became too ill to walk the stairs to his basement workshop. After Dad died, Mom remained in the house for as long as she could care for it, then sold it and retreated to an apartment that she thought safe and carefree.

Each time I visit my Iowa hometown I feel compelled to drive by 1604 East Street. In a neighborhood now fading, standing in the shadow of a high-rise interstate leg, the house seems to have shrunk since I lived there. The front porch seems smaller now than it did when we three sat drinking lemonade, catching the breeze on hot August evenings. The driveway seems shorter now than it was when I had to shovel it after school on gray, bitterly cold afternoons. Everything about the property seems now to have diminished except my regard for the man who dreamed this home and then applied his consummate skill, his patience, and his ideal of perfection to building it for us.

# *Tending a Child's Garden*

*You, too, my mother, read my rhymes,*
*For love of unforgotten times;*
*And you may chance to hear once more*
*The little feet along the floor.*

Robert Louis Stevenson

S ometimes I accompanied my father when he went to some of his customers' homes to collect overdue accounts. He ran a Standard Oil filling station throughout most of the Depression and all of World War II, a time when businesses in Cedar Falls, Iowa, were accustomed to extending credit to their neighbors. For whatever reason, however, some customers did not pay their bills promptly, and, after payment was overdue for several months, Dad had to knock on doors.

I did not accompany him to those doors, of course. I sat in the car, often reading a book. I would sometimes rather listen to the radio, but Dad insisted that would run down the battery, so I read or watched the birds or just waited.

One summer evening after supper, we drove to a house on the corner of Ninth and State Streets. Dad went to the front door, his account book in hand, where his customer met him and invited him in. Whether Dad emerged later with a payment on account or not, I do not know. I know only that he brought a book to the car when he returned.

"This is for you!" Dad said as he handed it to me. Perhaps the customer gave him the book in partial payment. I do not know. I was not accustomed to claiming any booty from such trips, so I must have been pleased to receive such an unexpected gift.

I could tell from the frayed cover that others had read this book before it came to me. Later, certain blemishes on the inside verified that first impression. The fact that the book was used did not make it any less valuable than a new book to me. I have always been interested to see how many dates are stamped on the inside of library books, delighted to find how large a community of readers has shared the book in my hand, how many other hands have turned its pages.

I studied the cover of this book: *A Child's Garden of Verses* by someone named Robert Louis Stevenson. A book of poems it was! I liked poems all right, but Mom usually read stories to me, stories like *Raggedy Ann and Andy*, *Amber*, and *Comrades of the Saddle*. On the cover of this book a girl in a yellow dress and a butterfly in a garden invited me inside. During Dad's next house call, I explored the inside of my new book. I liked the way the print lined up along the left margin, a capital letter standing boldly at the beginning of each line. I liked the wide margins, the generous white space on those pages. The illustrations captured my imagination immediately, black and white line drawings of children from another age enjoying things that I too enjoyed: walking in the rain, swinging, watching the stars, playing with boats and trains and toy soldiers.

Although I could read many of the poems in the Garden myself, I coaxed my mother to read my favorites to me over and over again at bedtime. Although she may have tired of them, I grew to love them like I loved my favorite songs. Soon, without effort, I had memorized some of them—learned them "by heart," a phrase I have always preferred—and recited them as Mom read them aloud, duets inspired by Mr. Stevenson.

*How do you like to go up in a swing,*
*Up in the air so blue?*
*Oh, I do think it the pleasantest thing*
*Ever a child can do!*

and

*A birdie with a yellow bill*
*Hopped upon the window-sill,*
*Cocked his shining eye, and said:*
*"Ain't you 'shamed, you sleepy-head!"*

and

*I have a little shadow that goes in and out with me,*
*And what can be the use of him is more than I can see.*
*He is very, very like me from the heels up to the head,*
*And I see him jump before me, when I jump into my*
*bed.*

Since then, that *Garden* has traveled with me to Cedar Rapids,

Iowa, and to Auburn, Alabama, sometimes living in boxes and trunks in hot attics, sometimes standing among other books of verse on my bookshelves. Time has frayed its cover even more, separated the pages from the binding. The first four pages are missing altogether, and others fall out each time I open the book.

Downsizing often means getting rid of books at our house, and
I enjoy giving them to friends or to the Friends of the Public Library for their annual sale. But I shall hold onto the *Garden* for as long as I have half an inch of shelf space to call my own. That book—and my mother—invited me to find joy and comfort in poetry, surely one of life's gifts to me.

# Friends and Neighbors

I am sitting on a little oak chair at the front of the classroom that I share with twenty-five other first graders. Only six of us are now sitting in the oak chairs carefully arranged in a semicircle at the front of the room. We are the Robins, and we are the best readers in the first grade at Manual Arts School. Miss Mary Hoagland, our teacher, will never say that, that we are the best readers. A kind person, she does not want to hurt the feelings of the Bluebirds and the Wrens, the vast multitudes now busy with their seatwork, waiting their turns in the reading circle.

Miss Hoagland takes her seat in front of us, her teacher's edition of *Friends and Neighbors* in one hand, a small stack of flashcards in the other. Before we read, we must warm up, like athletes do.

"What," says Miss Hoagland, "is this word?" She holds up the top flashcard in her stack. It is clearly *red*. We all know that word, having met it every day this week in our reading circle, but today my hand is the first one in the air.

"Terry?" she says, nodding in my direction.

"Red!" I declare with confidence, though not so loud as to disturb the Bluebirds and Wrens.

Miss Hoagland doesn't say "Right!" every time a Robin gets a word right. That would become tiresome for both teacher and Robin. Instead, before she moves on to the next word, she hands me the card with *red* printed on it, a token of victory to hold until the end of our reading lesson.

If learning is partly tactile, then I guess whoever invented those flashcards should get a medal. They are sizeable cards, each perhaps a foot long, with letters large enough to be read from the back of the classroom should that become necessary. But I like them most because they are constructed of heavy cream-colored paper, what I call "vanilla" paper until I learn later to call it more properly, "Manila" paper. I love the feel of flashcards in my hand, substantial and cool, and I crave more, more, more, the pure weight of them signaling my superiority as a reader.

Today, while the other Robins are reading their paragraphs aloud, I examine the cards that I have won: *red* and *ball, look* and *run.* I admire the crisp font in which they are printed, the one that the editors at Scott, Foresman have selected for the stories in *Friends and Neighbors.* They look exactly the way they look on the pages of the stories we have read this week. I am proud of my observation, tracing with my finger the *a* in *ball*, which doesn't look at all like the *a's* we practice printing every day.

I place the flashcards in my lap when it's my turn to read aloud about Dick and Jane. They have a new ball today, it seems—a red ball—and Spot, their dog, tries to snatch the ball when Dick and Jane toss it back and forth.  Spot is a cocker spaniel.  I wish I had a cocker spaniel at home instead of a turtle.  Turtles are no fun when it comes to playing ball.  Miss Hoagland allows me to read two whole pages.  She interrupts our reading only to correct our mistakes, and today she sits silently while I read.  I am proud.

Too soon our time in the reading circle ends, and the Bluebirds come to roost where we have made such rapid progress.  They are behind us Robins.  Before beginning my seatwork I hear them chirping for their flashcards, calling out words that we had called out two weeks ago.  Sometimes not even one Wren knows Miss Hoagland's word, and she has to help them.  I pity them.  There are more Wrens than either Robins or Bluebirds, and they are reading from a different book altogether, one with only a few words on each page.  I really feel sorry for them.

Today, for seatwork, Miss Hoagland asks us Robins to do page 16 in our *Think-and-Do* workbook.  Dick and Jane—and Spot!—are on p. 16, too.  They're not playing ball here, though.  They're doing something altogether different on this page, but most of the words are the same as the ones we just read in the reading circle.  After I read the directions, moving my lips only a little, I read the page, circling some words and drawing lines to connect others.  Where it tells me to copy words like *red* and *ball* several times at the bottom of the page, I try to make my letter *a* in *ball* look like the one in the book and the one printed in the orderly row of letters that march across the front of the room, over the blackboard, right above Miss Hoagland, who is now smiling at a Bluebird as she hands her a vanilla flashcard.

I love filling in the blanks on the workbook pages, printing my answers very carefully, tearing out my finished pages at the perforations, and placing them on Miss Hoagland's desk when the Wrens retire and reading lessons end. I really like getting those pages back the next day, too, especially when Miss Hoagland writes something nice at the top. (I like "Good work, Terry!" best. It makes me smile.) I also like taking the pages home to show Mom and Dad, who seem quite happy that I am a Robin, that Miss Hoagland thinks I do good work, and that I like being new in Dick and Jane's neighborhood.

# *Art and Soles*

It's Thursday, art day in Miss Walker's second grade class. Art day is not my favorite day of the week by any means, for that is the day that Miss Soles, the school district's only elementary art teacher, takes over for Miss Walker for the better part of an hour. For me, it seems an hour wasted. I dislike art class. I love looking at pictures in books and talking about them with my mother, but I hate doing art at school.

One thing about Miss Soles does intrigue me, though: her first name. I pride myself in learning my teachers' first names, although I would never call them by their first names, even at play. I enjoy collecting and remembering my teachers' whole names. My kindergarten teacher was the beautiful and kind Yvonne McGrane; my first grade teacher, down-to-business Mary Hoagland. Miss Walker has three names, all of which she signed on my report card: Inez Margaret Walker.

Miss Soles is a Vera. I know only one other Vera, Vera Haurum, my mother's friend, a happy woman whose sparkling laughter makes other people happy. But I think that Vera Soles is not a happy woman. She never smiles. In fact, she almost always wears a frown when she enters our classroom, lugging her supplies for the day, and she carries that same frown out the door when she leaves, our masterpieces in tow.

Vera Soles is standing next to my desk right now, frowning down at what she sees, her lips pursed as if she is thinking deep thoughts.

"What is that?" she demands, pointing to the narrow band of blue that I have drawn across the top of my page.

"That's the sky!" I reply, hoping that is what she sees, too. What else could it be, a narrow blue band across the top of my picture, right above the tree?

"That's not the way the sky looks," she barks. "Look outside!"

I do look outside, across the playground, across State Street, past David Stanard's house, to the trees beyond. Then I look up. Sure enough, there is the sky, right above the trees, just as I have drawn it.

"Color all of this white space blue," Vera Soles demands, tapping her right index finger on the white space 'twixt grass and sky. Then, without pausing for a breath, she says, "And you need to look at trees more closely, too. Do the tops of those trees out there really look like circles to you?"

I look outside again—same playground, same sky, same trees, which look pretty round to me.

I pick up my blue Crayola and dutifully begin to fill in the blanks on my drawing.

Vera Soles takes her frown to Shirley Nielsen's desk.

# Giving Grandma a Hand

"**L**et me see your hands, Terry."

I had joined my Grandma Ley for wake-up time in her bedroom one morning while visiting her and Aunt Helen in Los Angeles during the summer I was ten. I lay beside her on her double bed, both of us still in our pajamas. The California sun shone through the two windows over the headboard.

I offered my right hand. Why did she want to see it?

She placed my hand palm on the back of her own right hand. She lifted both into the warm sunshine so that we could see them clearly.

I saw her stubby fingers, her well-trimmed nails. I saw prominent blue veins, rough skin, wrinkles, liver spots, enlarged knuckles, a white scar at the bottom of her thumb.

I saw none of these things on my own small hand. Although my fingers were long for someone my age, I thought them pudgy, like the rest of me. I chewed my fingernails then, too, so they weren't very nice to look at. And I saw no blue veins, no rough skin, no wrinkles, no liver spots, no scars.

Instead of calling me out for chewing my fingernails, as my mother often did, Grandma commented on something I hadn't thought much about then.

"You haven't done much hard work, have you, Terry?" she asked.

I guessed I hadn't. I had helped Dad some while he was building our house, but mostly to hold measuring tapes, pick up stray nails from a work area, or carry supplies to the car from the lumberyard. Sometimes I helped to shovel the driveway if Dad hadn't already shoveled it before he went to work in the morning. Otherwise, I used my hands to hold books, to write paragraphs, to fill blanks on workbook pages, to practice for my accordion lessons.

I hesitated before responding. "No, I haven't," I said then. I was embarrassed, I guess, not to show signs of hard work. The contrast in our two hands was so great!

"Someday, your hands will look a lot like mine," she said as she placed her other hand on top of my right hand.

Since that morning I have learned more about my grandmother. That morning in Los Angeles, her hands told a story that I could not yet comprehend or appreciate. Grandma Ley grew up on an Iowa farm. She married a farmer, and she worked hard as a farmer's wife and the mother of five children. When my grandfather was diagnosed with tuberculosis while still in his thirties, she had to do double duty as farmer and parent while Grandpa Ley convalesced in a sanatorium in Colorado. Her letters to him assured him that the farm work was getting done, that the children were healthy and reasonably happy. She missed him and longed for his return. She wrote nothing of her concern for making ends meet or her fear that he might not recover.

Grandpa needed more than the sanatorium could offer, though. He died the next year, leaving Grandma a widow with five children, one a newborn, and with few resources. Although some of Grandpa's siblings had ventured beyond their farms to become prosperous small-town bankers and car dealers, Grandma never realized any benefit from their wealth. Eventually she had to sell the farm and move to Cedar Falls, a college town where she could supplement what little income she had by providing board and room for students. A fine seamstress, she also took sewing jobs of all kinds in order to provide for her family.

During World War II, Grandma moved to Los Angeles with my two young, unmarried aunts, who had jobs in munitions plants. After Aunt Florence married, Grandma continued to live with Aunt Helen for the rest of her life—making a home for Aunt Helen and sewing for her "ladies" well into her eighties. She and I corresponded regularly as soon as I learned to write. In her letters to me, she wrote of homely things—the balmy weather in Culver City; her wee, apartment-sized garden; some gossip from one of her sewing customers; Aunt Helen's work as an accountant at Metro-Goldwyn-Mayer studios. Occasionally she wrote about a modest luxury—a new Easter hat, a movie she had seen, a Sunday afternoon at the beach at Santa Monica with Aunt Helen.

Sixty years later, I often remember that conversation with my grandmother when I have reason to look at my own hands. My hands have indeed changed, as she predicted. Now I see better fingernails but also prominent veins, deep wrinkles, folds of loose skin, some knuckles enlarged by rheumatism. They do resemble my grandmother's hands in some ways, but they tell a different story, a story of sedentary work, of softer tasks, of privilege.

Sometimes the shadows of regret and guilt creep in when I look at my hands, but, more often, I feel admiration and appreciation for those who preceded me, for those whose hands told different stories.

# *The Squeeze-Box and Me*

**M**aybe I wanted to take piano lessons because our
family so enjoyed gathering around Aunt Velma's
piano whenever she sat down to play for us when we
visited her family in Des Moines. We sang for an hour
or more each time, old songs and new, some singers having to
position themselves as close to the music as possible, to read
the lyrics of current "Your Hit Parade" favorites. I didn't try to
stand close for that reason because I had memorized many of
the lyrics by listening to the radio and to our modest record
collection. When I could stand close to Aunt Velma, I studied
not the sheet music but my aunt's hands as they glided over the
keys, her long fingers coaxing from that piano sounds that
invited us to sing together and, in doing so, to strengthen our
family bond.

I pestered my parents for piano lessons for some time
before my mother dealt directly with the issue when I was in
the fourth grade.

"Terry," she said, "our house is too small for a piano, and
we can't afford to buy a piano right now. What other

instruments would you like to learn to play?"

"Well...," I began thoughtfully, never having seriously considered playing anything but the piano, "I guess maybe the trumpet or the drums."

Mom hesitated when she heard those two alternatives, anticipating, I guess, the din in our house if I should actually become faithful in practicing either of those two instruments. Following a measure or two of silence, Mom gazed into my eyes, her lips pursed in thought. "How about the accordion?" she said hopefully.

How about the accordion, indeed? I considered my mother's suggestion. I guessed it looked a lot like a piano standing on end. The keys were black and white. Some fairly famous people, like Dick Contino and Gallarini and even Myron Floren, made their livings then entertaining people by playing their accordions. I could aspire to doing that.

As it turned out, at about the same time, my best friend Roger had been having a similar conversation with his mother, who just happened to be my mother's best friend. I suspect that our two mothers had conspired long before either Roger or I ever thought about playing accordions. Our scheming mothers, who soon arranged for us to begin our lessons in nearby Waterloo every Thursday afternoon after school, had caught us both in a squeeze play. We rode to Waterloo together, and our mothers enjoyed a one-hour gab session waiting for us while our teacher, Ann Moline, terrorized us. We alternated who would have his lesson first, figuring that Ann Moline would work out whatever peeves she had with the world that day on the first one having his lesson.

Each of us would eat his sack supper during the other's

lesson, but Ann Moline ate her supper while we were strapped into our accordions, spooked and sweating. While we struggled through etudes, missing sharps or flats, trying to give the impression that we had practiced more than we had that week, Ann Moline feasted on her beef sandwich, potato chips, and coffee. She paused long enough to swallow before chastising us verbally for missing notes or counting wrong. When we goofed, she would sometimes lay her sandwich on the music stand before reaching over to play the same measure or two on our accordions, perfectly, of course, but with greasy hands. After the shock of each lesson wore off, on the ride home, Roger and I often found humor in our agony and laughed and giggled until our mothers shushed us.

Although Roger and I both loved music, he was more talented than I in performing it, perhaps because he was more committed to practice. It didn't take long for Roger to move ahead of me. While he was playing "Melody Moments," I was still playing exercises and etudes; while I was playing "Melody Moments," he was playing "In the Hall of the Mountain King" (two sharps!). We graduated from beginners' twelve-bass-button accordions to adults' 120-bass-button accordions. After a couple of years, we abandoned Ann Moline and our weekly pilgrimages took us to a series of instructors at The Music Corner. I dreaded confrontations with music containing three or more sharps and flats. Getting me to practice a half hour each day became a greater struggle for my mother as time went by.

I couldn't help wondering where my career as an accordionist would end. As the months and years went by, I became quite certain that my destiny would not be stardom. I surely didn't sound anything like Dick Contino, who had recently won *The Original Amateur Hour* contest and the hearts of every female who had seen his publicity photos. Heck, I didn't even sound much like Roger—and, frankly, I didn't always think he sounded so hot. Dick Contino's signature song was "Lady of Spain," a rousing tune made even more exciting by his ability to perform it with "bellow-shakes," a unique sound created by shaking one's accordion's bellows while playing whatever tune was at hand. Learning to play "Lady of Spain" with bellow-shakes became my ultimate goal as an accordionist—and the point at which I planned to make my grand exit from the accordion arena, withdrawing from the competition.

Reaching my goal was not easy. I had to convince my current teacher to assign me "Lady of Spain" in the first place. Then I had to buy a copy of the music (with Dick Contino's smiling face on the cover, to encourage and sustain me). After dealing with the initial shock of finding that my ticket to the mountaintop was written in four sharps, I had to withstand the agony of picking my way through that land-mined field the first twenty or thirty times. Ironically, my mother suffered with me throughout this process, for I usually practiced in the kitchen while she was preparing supper. How she kept a straight face after I learned all the notes and experimented with shaking my bellows, I do not know, but I suspect that she knew the end was near, and that sustained her.

Several weeks after I began my campaign, I proudly played "Lady of Spain" with bellow shakes for my teacher, who, unimpressed, nodded and uttered something like "Okay" before assigning my next piece. There weren't many assignments for me after that. After "Lady of Spain," I found my mother quite willing to allow me to forsake the accordion in order to pursue other interests—our church's choir, my part-time job, our junior high school newspaper. We retired the accordion to the attic, where it languished for several years, unplayed, until I seized the first opportunity that I had to sell it.

Although the accordion is gone, the melody lingers on. Learning to read music has served me well as a choir member throughout my life. Struggling to perfect my own performance of even the simplest songs has made me appreciate other, more skillful musicians—and to seek them out as often as possible. And I will always love "Lady of Spain," regardless of who performs it, for it reminds me that, once, for about five minutes, I stood at the top of the mountain, successfully managing four sharps and shaking my bellows at the same time, smiling the smile of the liberated.

# Keys to My Future

Idesperately wanted to own the used Royal portable
typewriter that I saw in the window of the Waterloo
Typewriter Exchange. I visited it regularly whenever I rode
the trolley to downtown Waterloo the summer I was eleven
years old. The sign next to it boldly declared that I would need
$65 to take it home with me, though, and I surely did not
possess such riches. At least once I ventured inside the store,
where a kind salesman took the typewriter out of the window
for me to examine, to touch its black case, to exercise its
carriage return, to brush my fingers across its bold-lettered
keys. I assured him that I would return to buy it. I could not
tell him when.

At home, I declared my intention to buy that typewriter
and began to save what I could from my allowance and from
odd jobs for my parents, but by Christmas the investment
capital I had accumulated fell despairingly short of my goal. I
still needed $20 to make that Royal typewriter mine, and I
feared that someone else would snatch it out of the store
window before I could. My mother undoubtedly appreciated

my desire for the machine. She had watched my concentrated play with a toy typewriter that I owned when I was very young and, when I was in sixth grade, my fascination with a toy printing press, the instrument that allowed friend Beverly Pollock and me to publish occasional editions of *The Hollywood Star News* for friends who were movie fans.

On Christmas Eve, at my Aunt Velma and Uncle Chuck's house in Des Moines, I made my joyful way through a generous stack of gifts: a wool sweater, a pair of flannel pajamas, books (always books!), and (always) a box of stationery from my Grandma Ley, with whom I shared a continuing correspondence. Perhaps because I felt that good things often come in small boxes, I saved one of the smallest in my stack for last, a gift from my mother. The box was heavier than I expected, beautifully wrapped, as all of my mother's gifts were. What could it hold?

What it held were four rolls of dimes that my mother had saved for me since the summer before, the $20 that I needed to make that Royal portable typewriter mine.

On the first business day after we returned home from Des Moines, my dad drove me to the Waterloo Typewriter Exchange. I approached the display window anxiously, hoping that my typewriter would still be there.

It was.

I counted out the $65 for the typewriter and some additional holiday gift cash for a book that would teach me how to type.

With my mother's encouragement, I studied touch typing for the week of Christmas break that remained. By now an office worker herself who relied on her typewriter, my mother insisted that I learn to type properly. Mom covered the keys with tiny bits of adhesive tape, so I couldn't peek at the keyboard. (I wondered why the inventor of the typewriter didn't just put the keys in alphabetical order.) I practiced daily, assisted by the stand-up model of a typewriter keyboard in my book. During that intensive touch typing boot camp, I worked my way through a big stack of inexpensive newsprint, copying articles from the newspaper and poems from *A Child's Garden of Verses*. Then, feeling confident, I typed thank you notes for Christmas gifts and my first typewritten letter to my Grandma Ley.

Emma Jane Hobson, my seventh grade English teacher, had assigned a short essay just before our holiday break. I don't recall the assignment, but I do remember writing the paper in pencil first, then typing it carefully (perfectly!) to deliver into Mrs. Hobson's hands on the day I returned to school.

I respected Mrs. Hobson; after all, she had richly rewarded me for diagramming what seemed like an endless procession of sentences, on notebook paper and on her blackboard. But I couldn't bring myself to like Mrs. Hobson very much because she seldom smiled; indeed, she wore a perpetual scowl that occupied her forehead, her brows, her eyes, her cheeks, and (I swear!) even her chin. She seemed to approve of nothing.

Before class began the following day, Mrs. Hobson approached my desk, her scowl directed at me. "Terry, what is this?" she said, waving my typewritten essay at me.

"It's my essay, Mrs. Hobson," I said, knowing that surely I had not forgotten to type my name at the top.

"Did your mother write this for you?" she snarled, tossing my essay on my desktop. Apparently she was not accustomed to receiving typewritten papers from seventh graders, but I was not accustomed to being accused of cheating, either. I sat silent, my face and ears turning crimson in embarrassment.

Finally, after what seemed an age, I worked up the courage to defend myself. "I got a typewriter for Christmas," I explained, "and my mother helped me learn to type." It was Mrs. Hobson's turn to remain silent while she considered how to deal with the situation.

"Good. If that *is* the case, bring a note from your mother," she said, turning on her heel, scowl intact, and shuffled off to harass another classmate.

Although Emma Jane Hobson passed out of my life at the end of seventh grade, that used Royal portable and I remained companions for many years. Together we wrote articles for junior high and high school newspapers that I edited. We wrote a senior term paper on British education. We wrote analyses of plays, poems, and novels for college classes. We wrote letters to my grandmother and to my parents. Later, that Royal yielded to a fancier new Smith-Corona portable electric and, eventually, to my first computer, but no instrument held the keys to my future quite like that used Royal portable did.

# A Lamme's Tale

When I entered the tenth grade at Cedar Falls High School, I looked forward to meeting three women who had been my mother's teachers when she was a student there. I had seen Miss Rait and Miss Abell at church, for they were Presbyterians, as I was, and they often sat together. Margaret Rait taught advanced algebra, and Marietta Abell taught senior social studies. I did not know Blythe Lamme at all, but I actually met her first because she taught World History to all of us sophomores.

Although I had generally enjoyed being a student, social studies had not been my favorite subject, probably because of the way it was so frequently taught: a chapter assigned and read; a battery of objective, picky questions answered by filling in blanks, often followed by long sessions of "going over" our responses and quibbling about correct answers; and a unit examination that primarily tested our memories. In those days, our success in social studies was measured by percentage points reflecting only the number of "right" answers that we supplied. Course objectives apparently did not include

40

developing students' imaginations or their critical thinking skills. That I had succeeded in previous experiences with the social studies can probably be attributed to my will to succeed, surely not to my love for the study of history or civics!

Having such previous experiences with social studies under my belt, I predicted more of the same in World History. On that September afternoon I took a deep breath and entered Miss Lamme's classroom.

Miss Lamme was seated at her desk, a large woman in a tweed suit and sensible shoes. Her salt-and-pepper hair was cut short. Later I observed that she was her own hair stylist, arranging it frequently by running her hands through it as she spoke. She wore large glasses with thick lenses, the better to see us with, though she often closed her eyes while speaking.

I was surprised to see Miss Lamme's room arrangement, a most unusual one at CFHS: The armchair desks arranged in parallel semicircles facing Miss Lamme's desk. Seated in the middle of the back row, I could see almost all of my classmates' faces, not just the backs of their heads, a real novelty. From my vantage point I observed the room's Spartan décor. A small battalion of roll-up maps were stationed above the blackboard at the front of the room. On the bulletin board near the door Miss Lamme had posted utilitarian notices regarding lunch schedules and fire drills, but little else. The bookshelves that ran the length of the room, below the bank of windows, were sparsely inhabited. I looked about me for stacks of thick history textbooks that Miss Lamme would issue to us on that first day, but I saw none. Perhaps she would bring them from a storeroom to issue tomorrow.

During that first class period, Miss Lamme talked about

what history is (surely I already knew that by now!), told us how important contributing to class discussions would be and how she would grade our work. She also described a Very Important Scrapbook Project that we would be working on during that first semester. She said nothing about readings from our textbook. Toward the end of that period, instead of issuing textbooks, Miss Lamme distributed a single-page worksheet. As the stack of worksheets made its way toward me, I watched classmates inhale deeply as they held the stack, savoring the aroma of duplicating fluid that clung to it. With a submissive sigh I reached for the first of what would surely become a giant stack of worksheets for World History.

I was shocked by what I saw when I examined the page. It contained a dozen purple questions, all of them quite abstract, I thought: How do historians define *history*? Where do two authors on your reading list begin their accounts of world history? What are the copyright dates for two of the books on our reading list? Why are those dates important? What are hieroglyphics, and why are they important to world history? I awaited Miss Lamme's defense of this most unusual assignment.

She began, "I'll not be giving you a textbook for World History." She paused for our collective sigh of relief, undoubtedly amused by the smiles that followed. She continued. "Instead, I'll require that you read about world history from the books on the shelves in here and a collection of textbooks on reserve for you in the library and the study hall. You'll spend the class period tomorrow reading from the books here, seeking answers to the questions I have given you. Before class time on the following day, you are to examine additional resources from those listed on the handout and be prepared to participate in small group discussions of the questions." Oops! If we could have retracted our sighs of relief, our smiles of liberation, we would have. This did not sound easy.

And it wasn't.

Each week, Miss Lamme distributed a new assignment sheet, each one containing ten or twelve questions to guide our reading in at least two of the historical sources that we chose from her list, most often history tomes. I tried to use my class time productively during study periods, and I frequently joined the rush to the librarian's reserve desk at the beginnings of study halls, hoping to glean enough information to satisfy Miss Lamme and to be able to participate in whole-class and small group discussions of the week's topic. I read a lot of history that year—and, I must admit, I acquired skimming and scanning skills that have benefited me ever since.

I would be exaggerating to say that our discussions were always compelling that year. They were indeed sometimes tedious, even (dare I say?) boring. However, they were also sometimes stimulating, even (dare I say?) combative, especially when we discovered that our sources didn't always agree with each other! Although dates and names seemed consistent enough among our sources, we often found the historians at odds over causes, motives, and resolutions. Although we reread and compared passages, we often could not determine which historian was "right." On those days, history became a puzzle, an unsolved mystery, that intrigued me.

I probably carried away a mere thimbleful of what Miss Lamme hoped that I would learn about the Phoenicians, the Roman Empire, and the Crusades while I was a sophomore. I was too young then to appreciate Miss Lamme's gift to me;

indeed, I was not consciously aware of it until I started my own research for my doctoral dissertation. Alone in a library carrel at the University of Iowa or at my desk at home, I pored over the scholarly work of others who were interested in my field of study and had contributed to it. They did not always agree. They forced me to reread what they had written, to compare their works with a critical eye, and, finally, to draw reasonable conclusions before proceeding. How like Miss Lamme's World History class this is, I thought. By not issuing a single history textbook, by forcing me to read diverse accounts of the same events, and by providing opportunities for me to compare my perceptions with classmates Miss Lamme had not only helped me to understand history and historians but also to tolerate ambiguity in the real events and the experiences that I would encounter throughout my life.

# Solo Fright

I have always loved music and singing. At every opportunity, my Aunt Helen reminded me and anyone within earshot that, at three, I knew all the words to "Jesus Loves Me" and sang them with gusto at the Baptist Sunday school where she often took me. During World War II, when my Aunt Darlene lived nearby, at my grandmother's house, while my uncle was overseas, I planned to be in Grandma's dining room when it was time for my baby cousin's nap, for Aunt Darlene always sang as she rocked Rickey to sleep, a copy of *Hit Parader* magazine in one hand. That fortunate child went to sleep with the lyrics of current pop tunes lingering in his tiny ears!

At home, Mom and I listened to *Your Hit Parade* on radio every Saturday night, often predicting the songs that would be #1 and singing along with Snooky Lanson or Dorothy Collins. I treasured the children's records that I bought with gift money and wore white and scratchy with repeated playing. In those days, some of the most exciting shopping that I did was with my mother, on those rare occasions when she took me to the small music store downtown, to choose a new record. We usually agreed on which recording of a Hit Parade song to buy, carried it home very carefully, for records were fragile then, and played it again and again, until we had memorized the lyrics not only of the popular "A" side but also of the "B" side that we rarely heard on the radio. Our family's modest record collection eventually provided me with the raw materials for my solitary play as a disc jockey, an imaginary career that spanned at least four years of my young life. I still want to be a disc jockey in my next life.

As I grew, I enjoyed the opportunities that I had to sing, in music classes, in school choruses and vocal ensembles, and in our church choir. I suppose that I had a fair voice but nothing to write home about. Although I often fantasized scenes in which I was a pop vocalist, adored, in real life no one asked me to sing a solo until I was a junior in high school, when Mr. Evenson, our choral director, asked me to sing a solo with the concert choir for the spring concert, when the choir, accompanied by the concert band, would close the concert performing Fred Waring's dynamic arrangement of "The Battle Hymn of the Republic." Mr. Evenson asked me to sing the second verse. I was delighted, of course, because, finally, someone had detected my latent superstar qualities and was giving me my Big Chance.

I worked very hard to be ready for my public debut. At home, I sang "I have seen them in the watchfires of a hundred circling camps…" a hundred times. After lunch each day, I retired to a music practice room with my girlfriend, Mary Lou, who played piano. There, I sang "They have builded Him an altar in the evening dews and damps…" another hundred times, caressing each note as lovingly as I thought it decent for a young man to caress notes in public. By the day of our dress rehearsal and performance, Mary Lou needed no music to accompany me, and she pronounced me "Ready!" Mom and Dad surely must also have been convinced that I was ready.

At dress rehearsal in the gymnasium, during choir rehearsal time, Mr. Evenson gave me instructions for my part of the production. Near the end of the first verse, the choir would part, and I would leave my position among the basses on the risers and walk to the spotlight in the center of the gymnasium floor, render my solo while the choir (now my backup singers!) sang "Lu-lu-lu" in the background. After singing "His day is marching on," I was to turn and walk behind the choir while the choir sang the third verse, ending the concert.

Naturally, I was nervous just before the concert. The gymnasium was overflowing. Not only the bleachers but also the chairs set up on the gym floor itself were occupied. Mom and Dad were among the crowd. Although it was not unusual for Mom to attend school events, such visits were rare for Dad. As we took our places on the risers, I tried to locate them in the crowd, but the gym was extremely dark except for the spotlights focused on us, so I could not see them. However, at the rim of light, seated in the front row, sat Mrs. Struyk, our school's senior English teacher and sponsor of the newspaper staff. I liked Mrs. Struyk, who looked as if she was enjoying the evening.

When it was time for the evening's finale, the tympani rolled, the band played the dramatic opening of "The Battle Hymn," and we were off, fully intending to chill the bones of an adoring audience. At the end of the first verse, on cue, my fellow singers parted to permit my passage to the gym floor, the follow-spot found me and directed my way to the center circle, and the choir began its "Lu-lu-lu," preparing the path for my solo.

Standing alone in the spotlight at the center circle, I concentrated on my entrance, pursed my lips to sing my first line. Having no other visible audience to sing to, I looked straight ahead, into the face of Mrs. Struyk, who smiled at me—and with her smile erased all memory of the words that I had so diligently rehearsed. The choir "lu-lu"ed right past my entrance. I remember thinking that I would enter late, sing the second line—but that line was soon gone as well. I stood, frozen, in the spotlight, my mouth open to emit words that would not come. As the choir finished its part of the second verse (a hundred or so "lu-lu"s), I closed my jaw, pivoted to my right, escaped the spotlight, and huddled behind the choir, where I remained, utterly humiliated, while the choir finished its grand finale without me.

I do not know how I escaped the gym when the lights came up and the other musicians made their way through the crowd and back to the music rooms. I don't remember what people said to me, if anyone spoke. I remember only sitting in the choir room alone after everyone else had gone, wishing I could get home without anyone seeing me, wishing I would never have to return to this school, this room. Eventually, my parents came to the door to claim me, and I fled into the night with them. What they said to me, I do not remember, but I'm sure they were kind, as they always were when I tried something new and didn't succeed immediately.

Unfortunately, my reaction to what I saw as a catastrophic failure was avoidance. The next day, I set into motion plans to avoid being reminded of my failure again and again in the future. I decided not to be in concert choir during my senior year—theoretically because, as editor of the school newspaper, I would need the choir rehearsal period for working on the newspaper, but mainly because I wanted to avoid painful reminders of one of my life's most embarrassing moments. Since then, I have avoided memorizing anything for public performance, fearing repetition of those awful minutes.

Asked to speak during the program at our high school class's fifty-year reunion, I reminded my classmates of what had been one of my life's most humbling experiences. I allowed as how I was fortunate, in a way, to have such an experience while so young. But, I said, I needed to finish some unfinished business.

I asked my classmates to sing "Lu-lu-lu" with fervor. They did!

And I sang the second verse of "The Battle Hymn of the Republic," from the podium, the lyrics printed on the card I held in my hand.

# Memory Gems for Uncluttered Minds

As we grow older we tend to trust our memories less and less. There was a day, though, when memorizing and remembering facts, lists, and statistics were child's play for us. We did it all the time. Our academic success depended on it! My junior and senior high school English teachers often required that we learn poetry "by heart"—and, if that weren't enough, we had to recite it in front of the class!

My junior English teacher, Mrs. Ella Mae Heide, was infamous for her "Memory Gems," most of them stanzas from American poetry. Sometimes we recited our lines for the class, sometimes we wrote them out (yes, spelling and punctuation counted!), and sometimes (oh, pain!) we had to recite them for Mrs. Heide, sitting and sweating next to her at her desk. For the Memory Gem portion of our semester examination, we went to her desk, one by one, sat uncomfortably on the edge of our chair, drew a slip of paper from a box, and recited portions of whatever poem we drew. Some of us drew this one, from

William Cullen Bryant's "Thanatopsis":

> *To him who in the love of Nature holds*
> *Communion with her visible forms, she speaks*
> *A various language; for his gayer hours*
> *She has a voice of gladness, and a smile*
> *And eloquence of beauty, and she glides*
> *Into his darker musings, with a mild*
> *And healing sympathy, that steals away*
> *Their sharpness, ere he is aware.*

Others drew this one, from "What is So Rare as a Day in June" by James Russell Lowell:

> *And what is so rare as a day in June?*
> *Then, if ever, come perfect days;*
> *Then Heaven tries earth if it be in tune,*
> *And over it softly her warm ear lays;*
> *Whether we look, or whether we listen*
> *We hear life murmur, or see it glisten.*

But Mrs. Heide wasn't the only one who required memorization. In eighth grade, Lincoln School students recited Lincoln's Gettysburg Address for Mr. Charles Lindsey, our history teacher:

> *Four score and seven years ago, our fathers brought forth*
> *upon this continent a new nation: conceived in liberty, and*
> *dedicated to the proposition that all men are created equal.*
> *Now we are engaged in a great civil war. . .testing whether*
> *that nation, or any nation so conceived and so dedicated. . .*
> *can long endure. We are met on a great battlefield of that*
> *war.*

In ninth grade, for Mrs. Carolyn Pratt, who taught me both English and Latin, we learned Portia's famous speech from

Shakespeare's *Merchant of Venice* :

> *The quality of mercy is not strain'd,*
> *It droppeth as the gentle rain from heaven*
> *Upon the place beneath: it is twice blest;*
> *It blesseth him that gives and him that takes.*

We also recited lines from Longfellow's *Evangeline* that year:

> *This is the forest primeval. The murmuring pines and the hemlocks,*
> *Bearded with moss, and in garments green, indistinct in the twilight,*
> *Stand like Druids of eld, with voices sad and prophetic,*
> *Stand like harpers hoar, with beards that rest on their bosoms.*

Longfellow seemed a favorite of other teachers as well, for, along the way, we were obliged to learn these opening lines of his "The Village Blacksmith":

> *Under a spreading chestnut tree*
> *The village smithy stands;*
> *The smith, a mighty man is he,*
> *With large and sinewy hands;*
> *And the muscles of his brawny arms*
> *Are strong as iron bands.*

...and these lines from his "Song of Hiawatha":

> *By the shores of Gitche Gumee,*
> *By the shining Big-Sea-Water,*
> *Stood the wigwam of Nokomis,*
> *Daughter of the Moon, Nokomis.*

I always drafted my mother to be my partner in memorizing these texts, a task that she could not possibly have enjoyed because I was such a "slow study." I don't remember that she was impatient as we sat together at the kitchen table grinding out the memory process line by line, "beginning at the beginning" each time I added a new line or two, but I was surely impatient and, I suspect, pretty cranky. Because I had little heart for learning poems "by heart" as a youth, I seldom required my high school English students to memorize poetry for fear that the process would sour them on poetry altogether for life. Instead I was pleased when students chose memorization from the lists of options that I offered.

# Growing Up in Record Time

B ecause I loved music and enjoyed the records that my mother and I had collected over the years, I was excited when I learned that the tiny, vacant store near our favorite restaurant on Main Street in Cedar Falls would soon open as a music store, to be the only source for buying music in our town.

I do not know why I invented my dream to work in such a place. I was thirteen, quite satisfied with the weekly allowance that my parents gave me—enough for a movie, some popcorn, and a roll of Necco candy for Saturday movie matinees and an occasional afternoon at the Rollerdrome. But the more I thought about it, the more I thought it a dream worth pursuing.

My plan was to find someone working in the store before it opened to the public so that I could inquire about working there. A friend and I walked the mile or so from school to the store during long lunch hours. The first few times, we found the store empty, but one spring day we found a young man inside. How I worked up the courage to knock on the door I do not know, but when I did, I met the man who became my first employer.

A high school commercial subjects teacher who was realizing his own dream to bring music to his hometown, Keith Kuck must have seen something in me that he recognized as potential, perhaps my earnestness, my enthusiasm for music, my mastery of eighth grade English, or my willingness to work eight hours each Saturday for fifty cents an hour. He hired me, his only employee, although I could not work legally until my fourteenth birthday in May, shortly after he planned to open The Record Room.

I worked there for eight years, through high school and college, Saturdays and summer afternoons, extra hours at Christmastime. At first my primary task was waiting on customers. In those days that meant helping customers find the records they might want to purchase and, because there was no easy provision for customers to handle and listen to records themselves, I would "audition" records for them on a phonograph behind the counter. Demonstrating the new twelve-inch long-playing records required steady hands so as not to damage the records as I spotted as many tracks as customers wanted to hear before making their decisions.

In that regard, the customer I most dreaded to see walking into the store was Stan Wood, drama director at the college, because he would be seeking background music for his current production. When he walked toward the counter with eight or ten LPs in his arms, I knew it was going to be a long afternoon. And, although our profit was greater when we sold record players, I dreaded demonstrating our limited stock because it meant moving everything from the counter to accommodate whatever player I was demonstrating. Finding the proper replacement phonograph needle for a customer was tricky;

selling sheet music was a piece of cake.

I soon learned about marketing and profit-and-loss. The third summer I worked there, Keith returned to Northwestern University to work on his master's degree and left me in charge of purchasing, advertising, merchandising, and paying bills for the little store. (Should I order as many copies of "Autumn Leaves" as "Rock Around the Clock"?) Keith's mother, who knew little about the music business, worked mornings that summer; I worked afternoons and Saturdays. I could not help but feel a sense of ownership about the business. I found some joy in every sale. Each Saturday, at lunchtime, I walked to the First National Bank, where I deposited most of my meager check, keeping in cash enough to pay for my week's entertainment and to buy a record or two (maybe an LP album) for my collection.

Four years after opening The Record Room, when he saw that the store would never support him fully, Keith took a teaching job in Indianapolis and sold the store to the Teigelers. Then a freshman in college, I became the manager of the store because Delma Teigeler knew no more about the music business than Keith's mother had. Delma's young daughter, Sandy, became our only part-time help. Until I graduated from college I assumed most management responsibilities for the little store, by this time earning the princely salary of a dollar an hour.

Working part-time at The Record Room throughout those eight years was easily one of the best experiences of my youth. Meeting and serving the public helped me to overcome an essential shyness around strangers that I had brought to my work when I was fourteen. I made friends of all ages, friendships based upon a shared delight in music. Because I owned an extensive collection of current hit records, I became the resident disc-jockey at sock hops at my high school. I wrote a record column for my college newspaper for three years. While auditioning records for thousands of customers I grew to appreciate musical genres that I had known little about; as my knowledge of and respect for jazz and classical music grew, so did my tolerance of country and western music. I learned a good bit about business and economics by being immersed in management as I was. And, although my parents provided my board and room throughout college, my salary savings allowed me to pay for everything else—my tuition, my books, my transportation—while preparing for a rewarding lifelong career as an educator.

On questionnaires I list the University of Northern Iowa and the University of Iowa when responding to questions about my education. But before I matriculated at either of those institutions my work at The Record Room provided a valuable head start for my adult life. I shall sing its alma mater (with gusto!) forever!

# Of Pebbles and Brooks

Having finished my first year of teaching high school English in Cedar Rapids, I planned to begin my graduate studies at the University of Iowa in nearby Iowa City, but my landlord changed my plans. He had sold the house in which I lived, and I would have to move at the end of the month.

Having nowhere else to go on such short notice, I went home for the summer, back to Cedar Falls, where I had earned my bachelor's degree at the University of Northern Iowa. Somewhat reluctantly, I chose to take my first graduate classes at my alma mater that summer rather than delay my studies a whole year when I would begin at the University of Iowa.

One sunny afternoon, after lunch, while heading toward my class in the Auditorium Building, I met one of my former professors, Norman Stageberg. Dr. Stageberg had made a valiant effort to teach me structural linguistics and modern American poetry, tasks he completed with limited success. I had been a whiz at Latin grammar in high school, but the "new grammar" puzzled me. I had few problems understanding what

Robert Frost wanted to tell me, but T. S. Eliot remained a man of mystery to me. Nevertheless I admired Dr. Stageberg, who taught energetically and with good (often salty) humor.

When he asked me how I had enjoyed my first year of teaching, I probably told him more than he wanted to know—about how much I loved teaching, my students, my colleagues, my school. I told him about two colleagues who had become my mentors, from whom I continued to learn about my profession.

"Have you ever thought about becoming a teacher educator, Terry?" he asked.

I didn't know what to say because, frankly, I thought I was doing well to aim for achieving a master's degree. I could envision myself being quite satisfied to teach high school English—in Cedar Rapids—for the rest of my career.

"Teaching teachers is important work," Dr. Stageberg said, "and I think you should consider it."

I must have looked startled because he and I had never talked about personal things like professional goals. That he assigned me high grades in his classes signaled his regard for my scholarship, but I had no idea that he was interested in what I would make of myself. What I took as a personal compliment embarrassed me.

Having received no response from me, Dr. Stageberg continued. "Teaching is like tossing a pebble into a brook that creates countless ripples outward. Teaching teachers is like tossing handfuls of pebbles in the brook, each pebble creating countless ripples outward." He paused, perhaps thinking about his own career. "It's very satisfying work, and I think you're well suited for it."

Our conversation ended soon after that. He headed for his lunch on The Hill, and I went to my class. I hope that I had the presence of mind to thank him for that conversation because his analogy helped to set my course for the future. It lodged in my mind as I taught my high school students and considered whether to seek a doctorate—and in what field. It lingered there as I chose to leave secondary school teaching and come to Alabama to be a teacher educator. I wanted to influence as many folks as possible, to lay in an arsenal of pebbles to toss into as many brooks as I would find.

I often shared Dr. Stageberg's analogy about teaching with the prospective English teachers in my English Education classes at Auburn. I could usually tell by their expressions, their nods of agreement, that they "got it" and that the image appealed to the idealism that drew them to study education in the first place.

Several years ago I was pleasantly surprised to receive an e-mail from Matt, a bright and conscientious young man who had made his way through my classes with great success a decade earlier. I was pleased to learn that Matt had found pleasure in teaching English in small high schools in both Alabama and Florida. Two years earlier, after his principal had observed and evaluated his teaching, he had asked Matt if he had ever considered becoming a principal. He encouraged Matt to consider it. Matt said that he remembered my story and Dr. Stageberg's analogy while he was considering his own future. If he was creating ripples by being a good teacher, how many more could he create by serving as a principal who could facilitate good teaching by supporting the teachers and students in his school? When he wrote to me, he had completed his master's degree in school administration and was about to become an assistant principal at a new high school in his district. Matt seemed excited about the handful of pebbles in his hand and the brook that lay just ahead.

I find Matt's story very encouraging, for it demonstrates the power of analogy and anecdote and confirms that our students are sometimes listening hard to what we say, filing it away somewhere for future use!

# A Stormy Beginning

O ur sunny June day turned cloudy at 2:00 p.m., two hours before our wedding. By 3:00, as I made my way to the church, it began to sprinkle. By the time Mrs. Corning cranked up the prelude on the wheezy organ, the rain began in earnest. Guests arrived damp, under umbrellas.

Once I arrived at the church I paid little attention to the weather outside. My internal weather was more than a little shaky. Roger, my best man, was a calming influence. As a drama director and director of a drum and bugle corps he knew how to conduct major productions without falling apart. Just before show time he volunteered to go into the sanctuary and turn on the wee cassette tape recorder hidden in the choir loft that I hoped would preserve the event for posterity.

I breathed deeply outside the door to the chancel where I waited with my male attendants. We were as handsome then as we ever would be, all at the same time: We were resplendent in black tuxedoes, gray vests, gray-and-black-striped ties, and patent leather shoes—everything rented, of course, except our underwear and socks. Roger assured me several times that, yes, he knew exactly where the ring was; he had not lost or misplaced it since the last time I had asked him. Besides my own breathing and our nervous exchanges, I heard the happy chatter of friends who were gathering in the sanctuary, mixed with the occasional cries of children present. I heard thunder, too, often very loud now, and close—and I saw flashes of lightning that lit even the shadowy corridor where we stood awaiting our cue.

Several minutes later, I stood at the head of the center aisle, facing the damp but smiling witnesses in the pews before me. I suppose I heard the violin solo and the reading from Gibran, but I don't remember them at all. Finally, when Mrs. Corning struck up "Trumpet Voluntary in D," I knew it was time to pay strictest attention to what was about to happen. It was getting serious. I watched first Dorothy, then Pat, and finally Kay Lynn make their way up the aisle and find their places. The congregation rose. Two people stood at the other end of the aisle. One of them was Harold Young, soon to be my father-in-law, but who was the other one, the woman on his arm, that woman in white? She didn't resemble anyone I knew! Her dress, her veil, her hairdo, even the way she walked, all conspired to create a mystery that solved itself only as they moved down the aisle toward me. I was relieved to learn that it was Mari after all, and she was lovely!

Mari and her father ended their journey beside me. We exchanged nervous smiles, relieved (finally) to be in this place at the appointed time. The "Voluntary" ended. Except for the clearing of throats customary when music ends in any sanctuary, it was silent.

And then lightning struck the church—or very near it, a

strike punctuated by a thundering ka-BOOM that shook the building.

After a brief, stunned silence, a child cried, "What was that?" and Rev. Haney, apparently undisturbed, pronounced, "Hear these words of the Lord Jesus Christ."

Believe me, I was listening! Was this an omen? Was the church on fire? Would we have to postpone—maybe even cancel—the wedding? Had I rented all these fancy clothes for nothing?

Mari claims that she was determined that this show would go on, even if we had to have the ceremony at the Women's Club, where we had scheduled the reception.

The church was not burning, as it turned out, although lightning had zapped my brother-in-law's car outside, and several friends who were seated in the balcony swore they saw lightning pass from Point A to Point B there.

After that startling fanfare, the show did go on—and on and on. Next June 28 we will celebrate our golden wedding anniversary.

We listen to the tape recording of our wedding on June 28 every year, always anticipating the crash of thunder that clearly marked the starting line of our marathon—and giggling when it happens. We're awake then, alert, ready to listen again to the vows that we took on that stormy afternoon in 1969.

# The Cursed Christmas Tree

I successfully avoided being the one to put the lights on a Christmas tree until the first Christmas that Mari and I were married. My mother had painstakingly done that job all the years that I lived at home, often taking a whole evening to do so. During the years that I shared an apartment with my friend Roger, he volunteered to arrange the lights if I would get the tree in its stand, ready for decorating.

Mari didn't make the task so easy for me. She did not volunteer to do that job. In fact, she said, her brown eyes doing a job on me, "Daddy always put the lights on the tree at home!" I was trapped, doomed to wage battle with all those twisted cords and sensitive bulbs that would not light.

The weather did not make the task any easier—or my mood any cheerier—that first year. The Friday night we set out to select our tree was bitterly cold, the wind whistling, announcing what Midwesterners call "bad weather." As we climbed out of our warm car, we put on our insulated gloves and wrapped our mufflers around our necks a second time. Crystals of frost had begun to form on the pine, cedar, and spruce trees that stood erectly in long lines before us. After a few minutes of inspecting the merchandise, our fingers began to tingle with onset frostbite, and we chose a likely blue spruce, paid a king's ransom for it, and bore Christmas home in the trunk.

The next morning, as I prepared to secure it in the new stand that we had bought, I was shocked to learn that we had adopted a tree that was decidedly disadvantaged, having a severe case of spinal curvature. Alone in our garage, I cut off as much of the trunk as I dared, hoping that it would stand tall and straight. But no matter how much I cut, no matter how I rearranged it in the stand, the tree leaned as if had been standing in a strong wind for a long time. We had hoped for a perfect Christmas tree, but we would have to mask the tree's deficiency with lights, colorful ornaments, and tinsel.

That afternoon, I learned a lot about arranging lights on a Christmas tree, lessons purchased with much frustration. I arranged lights, rearranged them, took off whole sets of lights and started again. I tested strings of lights, replaced bulbs. Once, I braved the weather to make a trip to the hardware store for more strings of lights. My patience wore thin, but I persisted. After a couple of hours, frustrated and wondering what kinds of marks my mother would give me for my efforts if she could see the results, I stood back to examine the aesthetic effects of my efforts. Not too bad. I turned out all the lights except the lights on the tree. Not too bad. We turned to boxes filled with ornaments and tinsel, anxious to make this misshapen lady the belle of the Christmas ball.

That night, we went to a gala holiday party. Since Mari was new in town, she was a little nervous about spending so much time with so many people whom she did not know well, people who had been my friends for several years. On our way to the party, she told me that she would just have a glass of scotch, something she could nurse for a long time. Apparently, she ran out of scotch more often than she was counting on, because by the time we drove home, she was showing emotional signs of someone who had imbibed more than usual. Once inside our apartment, she lay on the davenport, one foot on the solid ground to steady her universe. I turned on the Christmas tree lights. Returning from putting our coats away, I found Mari weeping as she lay looking at the Christmas tree.

"What's wrong, Mari?" I asked. Had things not gone well at the party? Had someone hurt her feelings? Had she decided that she didn't like my friends after all? Was she homesick? sad? regretful? "What's wrong?" I repeated.

"Well," she said, sniffing, dabbing at her tearful eyes, her left foot still planted solidly on the floor. "Daddy didn't swear at the Christmas tree when he put the lights on it! He always sang!"

So I was the culprit, the Grinch who contaminated the joy of my bride's Christmas! I apologized profusely, I think, and promised never to curse the Christmas tree again. Since then, I have drawn Christmas-tree-lights duty for nearly fifty years, and generally I have tried to abstain from any mean or ugly language around the Christmas tree when my wife—or the spirit of my wife's daddy—is within earshot.

# *Of Open Doors and Mentors*

T his is the power of the effective mentor. We continue to draw on their presence many years later. Their real influence, however, is in our continued transformation of ourselves. Their demonstrations were so powerful, we wished to experiment on our own.

Donald H. Graves, *How to Catch a Shark*

Mentors have been around for a long time. The word *mentor* has been around at least as long as we have been reading Homer, since the ninth century B.C., for Mentor was Odysseus's "wise and trusted counselor," whom he entrusted with the education of his son Telemachus. Although my thesaurus lists *teacher, headmaster, tutor, governess,* and *pedagogue* as synonyms, each of those terms shares only a portion of its meaning with *mentor*.

Traditionally, mentors and their mentees (or protégés) choose to develop learning and teaching relationships with each other, and they actively nurture those relationships, usually over time. Although both parties benefit from such relationships, protégés probably have the most to gain by observing and conferring with mentors who are older, wiser, more experienced, and willing to share their experience.

From the time that I committed to becoming a teacher to the day that I retired after a forty-year career in Iowa secondary schools and at Auburn University, I benefited greatly from professional relationships with at least four colleagues whose professional zeal and wise counsel made me a better teacher and a more productive educator.

No one opened more doors for me than Mildred Middleton, my supreme mentor and head cheerleader. Mildred was English language arts coordinator (K-12) for the Cedar Rapids, Iowa, schools throughout my tenure as a teacher in that system. She was singularly successful in that work; that is, she encouraged us to break old patterns, to envision and implement new ones that were startlingly different, and to take pride in our work. Mildred helped us to define our paths; insisted that we do the planning, the writing, and the piloting; and saw to it that we had the time and the resources that we needed. One of those resources was Dr. Robert Carlsen, professor of English and Education at the University of Iowa. With his leadership and her constant support, we built an integrative, constructivist strands curriculum in English language arts so strong that the State Department of Education later based its secondary English curriculum model on it. Although she could have been an empire builder, Mildred was not; instead, she accepted praise humbly and insisted that "her teachers" share the credit.

How or why I became one of "her teachers," I cannot say, but she was my mentor and close friend for more than fifty years, and even after we were both long retired, we "talked shop" whenever we were together. Whenever Mildred wanted to encourage me to take a step forward, to embrace a new experience, to take on a new challenge, she spoke of "opening doors," and that metaphor, perhaps more than any other, shaped our relationship. So often did she speak of opening doors for me that it became a point of humor for us. "Another open door, you say? Mildred, I'm not sure I have enough energy or time to walk through another door!"

But I rarely had the courage to resist—and, what lay beyond those open doors was almost always an experience that strengthened me in some way. Because I crossed those thresholds that Mildred ushered me to, I served as an officer in the Iowa Council of Teachers of English; studied rhetoric and composition at the government's expense at Iowa State University one summer; served on numerous committees to construct new English curricula for grades 7-12; wrote and supervised the writing of thematic units used at all three Cedar Rapids high schools; helped to organize the state's Advanced Standing Program, a partnership between English departments in large Iowa high schools and English departments at several of the state's colleges and universities—and served as its chair for two years; became the head of the English Department at Kennedy High School when it opened; applied for a sabbatical leave that would permit me to complete my doctoral course work; conducted dissertation research that involved more than 600 Cedar Rapids junior high and senior high school students; after my sabbatical, asked to be assigned to teach reading at McKinley Junior High School, partly because Mildred encouraged me to get junior high teaching experience before moving on. Mildred strongly urged me to pursue a second career, in teacher education, although it meant my leaving Cedar Rapids—not an altogether happy event for either of us.

Surely I have left out some opportunities, and perhaps I have passed through some of Mildred's open doors without even knowing that she had opened them for me.

After leaving Cedar Rapids for Auburn in 1974, I maintained a steady correspondence with Mildred, and we kept in touch by telephone. She continued to lend her support long distance. Each time I returned to Cedar Rapids, we met for lunch and a long chat. When I returned to Cedar Rapids to help celebrate Mildred's hundredth birthday several years ago I made an appointment to spend some time with her two days before the public reception that would honor her. I enjoyed stories of her experiences as a young teacher and as an inexperienced but determined coordinator. We reminisced about school experiences that we shared. We discussed the current state of public education in the United States—and probably could have solved its many problems if we had had a few more hours to talk about them. I left that meeting grateful not only for the doors she opened for me but also for the perspective that I carried through those doors, influenced and nurtured by Mildred's example, her encouragement, and the faith she had in my ability to accomplish well whatever challenge lay beyond the threshold.

Two days later, about two hundred friends and colleagues gathered to pay tribute to Mildred:  to shake her hand, to embrace her, to wish her well, to tell her how she influenced their lives, and then to share their "Mildred stories" with each other over punch and brownies. Not surprisingly, many of those stories sounded a lot like mine.

# The Homework Queen

Although I taught for forty years, I recall only one student asking for more homework. Maria was assigned to one of my ninth grade classes that pedagogues of the day called "slow-moving," a term surely inappropriate for the manner in which they exited the classroom when the bell rang. Class members were capable of learning what I taught, but it took them longer than it took students in other classes. Because I preferred to monitor and help students in Maria's class while they worked on tasks I assigned, I issued modest homework assignments only once or twice a week. However, I did ask them to devote at least two hours each week to personal reading. One day in late September, Maria lingered after the other slow-movers had stampeded out the door.

"How can I help you, Maria?" I asked.

"Mr. Ley," she began, "my mother and I wonder if maybe you could give me some more homework."

Stunned, I asked what sort of homework she had in mind.

"My mother thinks I need to study grammar more," she said. "Could you give me some grammar homework every week?"

Amazed by what I thought I had heard, I said, "Grammar? You want grammar exercises to do at home?"

"Uh-huh," she replied.

That was surely one unique request that I could fill! I possessed an arsenal of seldom-used grammar books, brand new workbooks, even some grammar games that I was pleased to loan Maria for her self-improvement project.

For several months, Maria dropped off her grammar homework and picked up a new assignment each Monday. She insisted that I mark her errors and give her a percentage grade for each week's effort. Sometimes we talked about concepts she didn't understand, but it soon became clear to me that Maria and her mother were collaborating on those grammar assignments and that her mother was a great help to Maria. I was pleased that grammar had become a common ground for communication between mother and daughter.

Her relationship with her mother provided a second vivid memory from the year that Maria was in my class. One aspect of the curriculum for her English class was a very practical one: completing forms similar to those they would complete in the world of work. To serve that objective in an authentic way, I obtained some actual job application forms from a local business, distributed them to the class, and asked students to finish them in class. I asked them to bring the forms to me for inspection when they thought they had finished.

Maria was among the first to submit her application. While she stood beside me, awaiting my assessment, I noted that she had printed her responses neatly and that she had provided her name, address, and phone number in the correct blanks. Where it asked for the name of her parent or guardian, she had printed "Mrs. Mary Armstrong." Where it asked for "relationship," Maria had written "I love my mother very much."

After reading her response, I smiled but did not meddle with Maria's interpretation of the question. If the job were mine to give, I would have hired Maria on the spot!

# Alabama Bound

" Have you ever been to Alabama?" my wife asked. She knew the answer, but I responded anyway.

"No."

"Will they pay your way?"

"Sure!" I said.

"Then what do you have to lose?"

Having completed my doctoral work, I looked forward to beginning the next phase of my teaching career, preferably by preparing teachers for English classrooms. The Placement Bureau at the University of Iowa, with Mari's help, would set me on the right path. On the bureau's questionnaire, I checked every directional option except the South. The South, still in the midst of civil rights strife, had gotten very bad press. Stories of George Wallace having stood in the schoolhouse door, forbidding entrance to African American students, cast images of a cultural barrier that I did not fancy, nor did Mari, who taught American government to high school seniors.

I had applied for three positions and had been interviewed for two of them, one in Chicago, the other at the University of Cincinnati. I was scheduled to interview at a teachers college in Pennsylvania the following month.

When Al Atkins called from Auburn, Alabama, he said that he had seen my papers at a convention in Chicago. He had an opening in English education that might be well served by my interest in secondary reading and my thirteen years of teaching secondary school English. Would I like to come to Auburn for an interview soon? I told him I would talk it over with my wife and get back in touch. That's when Mari encouraged me to take the leap. I called Al back and set the date.

I had some real doubts about the two positions I had interviewed for—a consultant's position at a very large high school district outside of Chicago, a lily-white district that was determined to stay that way, and at a university where I had to walk through areas burned during riots to get to my interview, a city that had released several hundred public school teachers the week before my interview. In neither case did I find my potential employers particularly kind or hospitable.

What I found at Auburn was open-hearted kindness and professional energy. One of my future colleagues offered to drive me back to the Columbus airport when my luggage finally arrived on a later flight than I had taken. He took me to dinner that evening and to breakfast the following morning, then monitored my two-day series of interviews with the faculty in Secondary Education, with individuals and small groups, and with the dean and his associates. The position open was ideal for me. While typical positions in English education permitted one to teach only a methods course and to supervise student teachers, this position would also permit me to teach a secondary reading course and a methods class in the teaching of linguistics and to consult with local schools wishing to expand their programs in secondary reading. When I left Auburn, Al promised to get back in touch with me after they interviewed one more candidate.

After serious discussion Mari and I agreed that the Auburn position would be the best one for us. We were willing to deal with cultural differences that we anticipated and that made us a little anxious. The following week, both Chicago and Cincinnati called to offer me their positions. Although I am often guided by the "bird in the hand..." proverb, I asked for a few days to make a decision. Because I had not yet heard anything from Auburn, I screwed up my courage and, during my preparation period at school, called Al Atkins. I told him that I had been offered two positions but was impressed by Auburn and wondered when Auburn might make a decision.

"Dr. Ley," he said, "Dean Pierce told me this morning that I can offer you the position."

That was April 1974. The people with whom I interviewed became warm friends and supportive colleagues. The position was all that I hoped for—and more, as our curriculum—and I— continued to grow. In our new environment Mari and I dealt with certain evolving cultural issues related to poverty, racism, injustice, and paternalism. Later, we rejected potential moves to Dallas, to North Carolina, to Utah, or back to Cedar Rapids. Over time, instead of remaining "home," Iowa became where we enjoy visiting beloved family and friends from time to time. We remain grateful for all that Iowa has given us—especially our educations and our opportunities to build careers—but Auburn and Auburn University became home.

We are indeed happily bound to Alabama!

# *Litany*

C lick. Click. Click-click.

Yvonne McGrane. Mary Hoagland. Margaret Inez Walker and Myrtle Young.

Click. Click.

Rosa Janssen. Dorcas I. Fuller.

It's only 9:30, and I have already learned something important about myself this morning: I am claustrophobic! The MRI machine that I'm attached to has taught me that. On the questionnaire I answered before this procedure, I said that I wasn't, and I didn't think I was. I have no trouble riding in elevators or being in rooms without windows. Come to think of it now, though, I have never liked having my head covered by blankets—or water! And I surely found no joy when I chose to hide in a pitch-dark closet during childhood games of hide-and-seek. Perhaps I have been claustrophobic all along and didn't know it. I think my body alerted my brain when the kind technician placed my head in a metal mask and fastened it to this glider that I'm riding back and forth, completely out of my control. I close my eyes. Can I forget where I am?

Click. Click. Click-click.

Joe Valenta. Lucille Creighton. Roger Romine and Charles Lindsey.

Click. Click.

Emma Jane Hobson. Carolyn Pratt.

Knowing that I must do something to take my mind off of my predicament and this chattering machine, I turn to all the teachers who have crossed my path. For some reason I always made it my business to learn my teachers' given and surnames—sometimes even their middle names or initials. Often their signatures on my report cards were all that I needed. Sometimes I had to do some detective work of my own, remaining alert to conversations between teachers when they were likely to use their given names.

Click. Click. Click-click.

Elizabeth Sullivan. Clarence Pries. Helen McDowell and Ella Mae Heide.

Click. Click.

Blythe Lamme. Lorraine Devereaux.

I begin at the beginning, with Yvonne McGrane, my kindergarten teacher, whom I loved but who abandoned me for another man before I entered the first grade. I recite their names to myself, shaping them to whatever poetic rhythm I can find. I pause slightly when I reach Lorraine Devereaux. She was young and beautiful but a terrible teacher of American history. I lose several beats in my litany, thinking about her, but then proceed to Francis Babcock, who gave me the only "C" I earned in high school, for geometry, a subject whose beauty entirely escaped me.

Click. Click. Click-click.

Norman Jespersen. Anton Hofstad. Dorothy Struyk and Marietta Abell.

Click. Click.

John Evenson. Merle Picht.

Having finished high school, I am ready for college—and more than ready for the machine to end its chatter. But it does not.

Click. Click. Click-click.

Norman Stageberg. Josef Fox. H. W. Reninger and Louise C. T. Forrest

Click. Click.

Howard VanderBeek. Robert Carlsen.

As I reach the end of my litany, the machine's powerful magnetic field is still reading my bones, my brain—not finished with its book report on what it has read. I pray for it to find resolution and end.

Click.

Yvonne McGrane...

And I am back to kindergarten.

# *Time for Retirement*

**M**aking plans to attend an afternoon retirement reception for three colleagues recently set me to remembering my own retirement years ago—an all-around joyous event. Colleagues congratulated me that day, and I basked in the glow. Former students wrote kind letters that I still read from time to time, and I warm to the afterglow. Some generous souls even sent gifts. I especially treasured the books and the bookstore gift cards, for I fully intended to read, read, read now that I had achieved emancipation.

But the clocks! Three friends gave me clocks—lovely clocks, I guess, two for my mantel and one for my desk. Curious gifts, these. What would I need with clocks now? I would surely no longer arise at 5:45 each morning, be dressed by 6:30, be bound for the office by 7:00! I would no longer have to race the clock to complete an ambitious lesson plan before the bell rings. I would no longer have to worry about being punctual for graduations or department meetings.

I understand giving timepieces to high school or college

graduates. What lies ahead of them is a minefield commanding punctuality. Having emerged from that minefield whole, however, I anticipated long mornings devoted to sipping coffee and reading two newspapers. However, I would constrain my urge to become utterly indolent by promising myself never to eat lunch in my pajamas, a promise that (pretty much) I have kept. I wasn't sure then that I would even need to wear a wristwatch post-retirement.

I wrote proper thank-you notes to the three clock donors, of course. My mother taught me to be gracious in acknowledging even gifts that I had absolutely no use for. (Note that I ended that sentence with a preposition, another luxury enjoyed by retired English teachers.) Mother told me to mention something unique or appealing about such gifts—to say that I was glad that the new pants didn't itch, say, or that the phosphorescent yellow sweatshirt was just the right size. How to say that I was grateful for clocks that I did not plan to use? Minutes ticked by as I sat with pen poised over the first blank card, awaiting the Thank-You Muse.

Finally the Muse arrived, and I wrote: "Thanks a lot for the beautiful retirement clock. It is beautiful, it keeps accurate time, and—best of all—it has no alarm!"

# *Songs of Literacy*

S hortly after I retired I volunteered to provide some literacy support for selected fourth and fifth graders at nearby Wrights Mill Road School, children chosen primarily because they could use some one-on-one time to shore up their reading and writing skills, their self-confidence, and their positive attitudes toward communicating. Since then, I have worked with more than seventy boys and girls, meeting each of them for a half-hour twice a month. Each child has a distinct personality, of course, and a unique set of needs. Each reaffirms what I thought I already knew about teaching; many contribute to my continuing post-graduate study of education.

Shauntoria was among my first tutees. She had a reputation among teachers that made me wary of her at first, but our first conversation set me at ease. She spoke gently, but with self-assurance. She told me that she loved to sing and dance—"mostly at church," she said, but she admitted that she and her friend often sang and danced when they were together. When I asked her if she would like to sing something for me, she did not hesitate to sing a verse of a favorite hymn. My first conversation with Shauntoria suggested that music might be a way "in" to her literacy development.

After that, I encouraged Shauntoria to read poems to me at nearly all of our sessions, and I read poems to her. We both enjoyed the music of poetry, especially poems by Shel Silverstein, and she especially liked those accompanied by vivid, often playful, illustrations in picture book poetry collections. One day, we chose poems in a collection by Langston Hughes to read to each other. I chose "Daybreak in Alabama," one of my favorite poems by any poet.

> *When I get to be a composer*
> *I'm gonna write me some music about*
> *Daybreak in Alabama*
> *And I'm gonna put the purtiest songs in it*
> *Rising out of the ground like a swamp mist*
> *And falling out of heaven like soft dew.*

When I finished, Shauntoria looked at me, wide-eyed.

"That could be a song!" she said.
"Why don't you sing it?" I suggested.

And she did, in her mellow church voice, creating her own melody and an appropriate tone, a performance sweet enough to render me (and, I think, Langston Hughes, had he been present) misty-eyed.

Each year, fifth graders at the school participate in a Wax Museum. Each child chooses a person, living or dead, to "become" for the Museum project. They read a biography or autobiography about their choice and develop a tri-fold display about him or her. On Wax Museum day, wearing appropriate costumes, they recite original three-minute speeches, assuming the point-of-view of their historic figure, for younger children in the school who visit the Museum.

When Shauntoria and I discussed her choice, I suggested that she consider becoming a famous singer or dancer. After we talked about several possibilities, she chose gospel singer Mahalia Jackson. Because she had never heard Mahalia sing, I brought one of my recordings to share with her. During the sessions that followed, she read to me from the biography that she chose, we collaborated to plan her speech, we talked about her graphic display, and she practiced her speech. On Wax Museum day, she delivered her speech with gusto, but also with the modest confidence with which Mahalia might have told her own life's story. The following week, she shared her teacher's evaluation form with me, justly proud of her success with a project that required reading, writing, art design, and performing.

This year, fourth-grader Cameron is highly motivated by weather. During our initial conversation he boldly declared that he will become a meteorologist and will move to Florida. Why Florida? Because there's a National Hurricane Center there! Cameron became intrigued by weather while reading a book about tornadoes and hurricanes. Although he is an avid fan of The Weather Channel and his weather radio, he also enjoys watching The Food Channel and helping his momma make red velvet cakes. I'm confident that Cameron can inform me about the weather. How can I engage the assistance of the weather to help him to become a better, more confident reader and writer?

# The Puritan Reader

I like to read before retiring at night, but most often I nap in my La-Z-Boy instead, wake up occasionally and read the same passages several times, and, finally, insert my bookmark (often in the wrong place) and toddle off to bed. I could blame this ritual on age, I suppose, but I'd rather place part of the blame on my mother.

My mother lived the Puritan work ethic and, by example and admonition, she made me her heir. On Mondays, she did the laundry before calling her friend Marcella for a long chat. On Tuesdays, she had to finish ironing before turning on the radio to hear *Stella Dallas* or *Pepper Young's Family*. She dusted every day, and her Electrolux was a constant companion. If she tended to her duties and did them well, she had little time for reading and no time for napping. Work before pleasure was her mantra.

Eat your broccoli before you get any dessert, she told me. Do your homework before you go outside to play. Set your Sunday school money aside before you go to the movies. Deposit something in your savings account whenever you cash your salary check at the bank.

No wonder I have typically delayed pleasure for duty throughout my adulthood! I thought that during my retirement, when my duties diminished, I could surely devote myself to pleasure. Because I have always counted reading as one of my greatest pleasures, I imagined consuming hundreds of books, stacks of articles—pleasant reading matter for which I would not be held accountable by anyone. I could turn pages while the bed went unmade and the bills unpaid.

Throughout my career I felt obligated to read first those texts related to my profession, thus scrutinizing the literary texts that I would teach (*Hamlet* again?), articles about how to motivate high school writers, and research reports about whether phonics or whole language procedures worked best in elementary reading classrooms. Because I chose young adult literature as one of my areas of specialization, I felt obligated to keep up as best I could with the flood of new titles every year. I brought professional questions to even that generally pleasant reading: Who might be interested in reading this book? Is it well written? Is this a book worth teaching to whole classes, or would it be better as independent reading? If I were teaching this book, what might I want to emphasize?

Meanwhile, the adult fiction and nonfiction that I longed to read for my own pleasure languished on my growing Shelf of Good Intentions, some of those books growing considerably older while waiting for my retirement.

But we Puritans find it difficult to change. Today, retired seventeen years, I still honor my mother's example, her admonitions. Too often, I make the bed, pay the bills, tend to correspondence, sweep the sidewalk, take the garbage to the curb, and visit the fitness center before I take my book to a silent corner of the night—and sleep.

# J. J. and the Mythical Creatures

Why J. J. was assigned to be one of "my readers" I do not know. For the fifteen years that I have offered literacy support for fourth and fifth graders at our neighborhood school, most have been struggling readers. Many have been what we in the trade sometimes call reluctant readers, reluctant because reading is an unsatisfying chore for them, a chore they avoid whenever possible. Because I meet my readers one-on-one for only half an hour every other Wednesday, I do not pretend to teach them to read; I leave that to the skillful and committed teachers who meet them every weekday. I think my job is to discover each reader's strengths, challenges, interests, and passions and to build on them, to move each reader from avoidance to tolerance for reading, perhaps headed toward enthusiasm for "planting seeds by reading" as a way of life.

I knew that J. J. was unique when, without provocation, he wove the terms *genre* and *metaphor* into our conversation as we became acquainted during our first session in September. That he used those terms surprised, pleased, and alerted me:

Working with this guy should turn out to be both fun and challenging!

During our second session he chose to read to me from *Haunted Hotels*, a picture book populated by ominous clients, including vampires, poltergeists, and werewolves. When I asked J. J. why he chose to read that book, he surprised me again: "Because I want to be a mythologist!" he said.

A mythologist? Were there such persons? I decided to explore. "As a mythologist, what would you do?" I asked.

"I want to study creatures, like Bigfoot and the Abominable Snowman, to find out if they are real," he said, with an "Of course!" gleam in his eyes. Sensing my interest, he said, "You name a kind of animal, and I'll tell you if I know that kind of creature."

After pausing to recall my extended but distant experience with Greek mythology in Mrs. Pratt's ninth grade English class, I said, "How about a bird?"

"Well," said J. J., "there's the griffin—but it's not all a bird, just its head and its wings."

"How about a dog?" I asked. He thought for a few seconds.

"There's Cerberus," he said. "That's the dog with three heads that guards the gates of Hell."

I knew then that J. J. was a very unusual kid, one whose passion for a topic about which I know relatively little I should try to nurture.

As he was leaving that day, he paused at the door and said, "Maybe when I leave every time you could assign me a creature to learn about."

No teacher passes up a request for homework. Since then, J. J. has conducted his own brand of independent research, using the Internet, television documentaries, and books from the school library to learn about and then tell me about different creatures, among them the cockatrice, satyrs, Scylla and Charybdis, Grendel, and the Cyclops. One week he said he would like to learn more about Odysseus's trials in *The Odyssey*. I anticipated hearing J. J.'s version of Odysseus's encounters with the Sirens, Circe, and the Lotus-Eaters during our next meeting.

Each time we met, J. J. read to me from a book that he had chosen for independent reading. Among them were *The Gremlin's Curse, Haunted Caves, The World's Deadliest Sharks, Spooky Schools,* and *The Abominable Snow Kid.*

Even budding mythologists conducting research on creatures sometimes lighten up. One Wednesday, after we had quizzed each other from a book of riddles that we found in our assigned space, J. J. said, "Maybe I could make up some riddles about creatures." I told him that I hoped he would try.

He did. The following Wednesday he brought these riddles to quiz me:

"What did Medusa's friend say about her dress?"

"It's hissstonishing!"

"What meat does a vampire hate?"

"Stake."

Yesterday, during our final time together, J. J. read aloud to me from the book that he brought, *Mighty, Mighty Monsters,* with animated expression for each character's speech. Then, while completing a brief year-end reading survey, he paused before filling in the blank to indicate how many books he had read during the school year to ask, "Is it okay if I put the infinity sign there?"

"Of course," I said, "so long as you try to live up to it!"

The final question asked him how many books he thinks he can read this summer.

J. J. set an ambitious goal for himself: 24, he wrote! Then, with *Mighty, Mighty Monsters* under his arm, he walked into summer.

# *Whistler's Son*

**M**y father had many talents. He built our house, for one thing, and he could administer first-aid successfully to almost anything mechanical, from our Ford coupe to my electric train. Unfortunately, I did not inherit any of those talents.

But Dad was also a whistler. He whistled unconsciously while he laid the cement blocks that formed our basement or drove my mother to the grocery store. He whistled loudly when it was time for me to come in from playing. He often whistled softly while filling out his "time sheets" each weeknight, at the kitchen table, so that John Deere would pay him on Friday. He could whistle by puckering his lips. He could whistle through his front teeth. By placing two fingers near his mouth, he could whistle so loudly that neighborhood dogs flocked to our yard. Sometimes I could identify the songs that he whistled, but often, I suspect, he was improvising.

I can't say that I admired his whistling then. Whistling was just another part of him that I took for granted. Some fathers could sing; some could recite poems. Mine whistled. A lot.

I seldom sought to imitate Dad's whistling. The only times that I remember attempting to whistle like him were the times that I tried to whistle through my fingers. I failed repeatedly, and that was that. I still can't do it.

When I became a whistler I cannot say, but people began mentioning it when I was in my twenties. "You sound happy today," they would say—or they would ask, "What is that song that you're whistling?" Since others have brought it to my attention, I have caught myself whistling everywhere, at all times of the day or evening, while working at my desk, taking out the garbage, doing the laundry, even while vacuuming. Sometimes I cease whistling when I become aware that I am doing it, but in recent years I have just noted what song I'm whistling and wondered how that song flew into my head and out through my lips.

Sometimes I unconsciously take my cue from songs that I hear on the radio or on one of my CDs. Frequently I whistle all day Friday one of the anthems I have rehearsed with our church choir on Thursday evening. I sometimes whistle melodies from television commercials in spite of myself. Before entering a restaurant for lunch today, I heard a woman summon her friend in the parking lot. Thirty seconds after she shouted "Laura!" I began whistling Laura's namesake tune. Most often, though, I cannot trace the immediate source of what I am whistling. During my half-hour walk through our neighborhood tonight, for instance, I found myself whistling "Walkin' My Baby Back Home" and "Peter Cottontail." For some reason, entering the shower seems to be my cue for whistling "How Long Has This Been Going On?" Usually I whistle very softly, to myself, but when I am in a jovial mood I sometimes turn up the volume. Others in the fitness center dressing room often hear me whistling loudly to celebrate the end of my workout.

I doubt that my whistling has much of a future, although I recently read about a young man from Virginia whose whistling has paid off. Chris Ullman has won the national and international whistling contests four times, whistled for the President, whistled with the National Symphony Orchestra, and whistled the national anthem at several NBA games. He has appeared on CNN, National Public Radio, and the *Today* show. He has made a CD. Once his whistling helped him to land a job that he wanted! Chris says that he got his start from his father, too; unlike my father, his whistled Gilbert and Sullivan tunes.

Ullman says he enjoys performing for an audience because whistling makes people happy. I can understand that. One day while browsing in a quaint bookstore in Montgomery, whistling softly, probably because I was surrounded by thousands of books, I was surprised when a gentleman touched me on the shoulder. I recognized him as one of the anchors for the nightly newscast that we always watched. "Excuse me," the celebrity said, "but I couldn't help hearing your whistling. Hearing someone whistle makes me happy. Not enough people whistle these days!"

I am convinced that whistling generally arises out of the whistler's happiness, too, that it is one way of expressing joy, spontaneously, privately or publicly. I am proud to be a whistler's son.

# Reading at a Snail's Pace

I love to read. I have read hundreds of books. I have taught reading and literature for half a century. I am a devoted, sometimes tiresome, advocate of reading. My mantra is "Plant a seed. Read." But I must live with a dark, dark debilitating secret: I read at a snail's pace.

Consider a book that I am reading now, *Life of Pi* by Yann Martel. I chose it because I admired the film based upon it and wondered how the print version of Pi's story might differ from the film version. When Thomas, our neighbor who is a sophomore at Auburn University—an avid reader all his life—loaned me his copy, I committed myself to the book. If snails could read, they would read this book faster than I am. I began the book a week ago, and I have read 106 pages of this 400-page book. It's easy, pleasant reading: short, narrative chapters; accessible vocabulary; an engaging style. Part of my problem, of course, is that I reserve quiet time just before going to bed for much of my personal reading. Too comfortable in my La-Z-Boy at midnight, I alternate reading and dozing, often rereading the same passages two or three times before I give up, insert my bookmark, and retire.

But even under better circumstances, when I steal daylight time for reading, I read too deliberately. It seems always to have been that way. Although my reading pace has been troublesome for much of my life, I have only recently begun to wonder why I read so slowly.

I think I can place the blame on three factors.

When I was in elementary school, learning to read and, later, reading to learn, our progress was too often determined by workbook pages, comprehension quizzes, and tests that required remembering literal details of the text. (*What material did the second pig use to build his house? List three causes of World War II.*) Because I valued high grades, I read cautiously, to soak up facts that might later earn me gold stars. I equated school success with careful reading that would enhance my stock of useful details. My success reinforced that acquired habit of reading slowly, whether the subject was literature or history or science.

When I chose to become an English major in college, I unknowingly committed to snail-paced readings of literary texts, from *Beowulf* to Virginia Woolf. Text analysis required reading the writers' lines numerous times, then reading between the lines, processing metaphors, symbols, diction, and style to come up with a comprehensive and critical interpretation that would satisfy (maybe even please) Dr. Reninger or Dr. Stageberg. What they called "close reading"— and rewarded with praise that soothed my ego and grades that would enhance my GPA—effectively slowed my reading even further and also made me an anxious reader.

Without knowing it, my own students contributed to my deliberate reading habits as well. During the forty years of my teaching career I read thousands of student essays, projects, exams, and doctoral dissertations. Too often I assumed the role of editor of pieces they submitted for evaluation. Although I knew that it was important to encourage and praise my students, I felt that I must also make them aware of their limitations, whether those limitations were matters of content, organization, style, or mechanics. How could they improve their writing without knowing their weaknesses? And as their teacher, how could I plan my teaching without knowing what I needed to emphasize? Because I knew that my students could not learn to write without writing often, I asked my 130 high school students to submit a piece of "finished" writing about every ten days. While they were becoming prolific writers, I spent evenings and weekends reading and marking their work, reading purposefully, writing in the margins, often reading selected papers a second time before assigning grades to them. Later, at Auburn University, doctoral dissertations required scrutinizing and commenting on multiple drafts of research reports that ran up to 300 pages long. In such cases, I had additional motivation for critical reading: My name went on the cover page of each dissertation as chair of the student's committee.

Deliberate reading has some benefits, of course. Now, retired, no longer taking comprehension tests or marking student work, I linger over passages to delight in a vivid image, an apt metaphor, authentic dialogue, a masterful sentence. But I also catch myself doing close readings of comic strips, admiring the cartoonist's sense of irony or wondering why Charles Schulz always put two periods at the ends of his

Peanuts characters' sentences.

And so it goes, as it has always gone. I maintain two Shelves of Good Intentions containing books that I look forward to reading, but my intentions outstrip my ability to process books quickly. The shelves grow longer and heavier. I select my books with care, settle into my La-Z-Boy, and savor what I am reading until my eyelids grow heavy. I wake from a catnap, place my bookmark in the book, regretting how little progress I have made, and go to bed. I'll finish the book tomorrow, I will!

# Staying in Tune

In Julius Lester's *Black Folktales*, antihero Stagolee is given the choice of spending his afterlife in either Heaven or Hell. After touring both sites, he chooses Hell. What tips the scale? There's a jukebox in Hell!

Stagolee's choice gives me pause. Faced with similar options, where would I choose to spend eternity?

I too would probably choose wherever the music is best. Of course, I am confident that since Stagolee's day Heaven, aware of its fierce competition, has added music—and not all of it ethereal, performed on harps.

Wherever I go, I must have music.

Whether I am greeted by St. Peter or by Cerberus, the three-headed Hound of Hell, let me hear Michael Buble sing "The Best is Yet to Come."

Whether the way be sunny or lit by fire and brimstone, let Tina Turner light my path.

Whether the streets are gold or burning coals, let Frank

Sinatra set my pace.

Whether the air I breathe be fair or foul, let me hear George Shearing's piano.

Whether my diet be ambrosia or spinach, let me hear Mantovani at mealtime.

Whether I be in the company of seraphim or demons, let me hear the Mormon Tabernacle Choir.

Whether I am wearing wings or carrying a trident, let me hear Mozart on Mondays, Wednesdays, and Fridays; Beethoven on the other four days—Bach on holidays.

I have been told that we can't take it with us, but I'm wondering if technology might help me rewrite that script. If I download a couple thousand of my favorite songs onto my iPod, why can't a friend slip the iPod into my casket, thus assuring a musical interlude at least until I find a way of refreshing the iPod's battery? And if I store my music on The Cloud and go the right direction, my tunes will be only a hop, skip, or jump away!

# *Thanksgiving Prayer*

D ear Lord, thank you for ordinary things: hot water for baths, aromatic soap to keep me clean, birds that wake me in the morning and feed outside my breakfast room window—and thank you for the senses to appreciate the ordinary things around me.

Thank you, too, for extraordinary things: for meals that nourish and satisfy me; for artists who brighten my every day with story and image and song; for builders and technicians who know more than I do about how to keep me safe and comfortable; and for the vision of predecessors who made it possible for me to retire with little worry about my next pension check. And thank you most especially for meatloaf, butter pecan ice cream, and popcorn.

Thank you for people who have touched my life in special ways: for my parents, Mari, and her parents, of course, but also for aunts, uncles, cousins, and close friends who extended my tiny family so richly. Thank you for leading me to a life dedicated to education and to mentors who opened doors and invited me through. Thank you for administrators and colleagues who encouraged my professional growth, and for so many receptive students whose responses allowed me to measure my own growth as I tended to theirs.

Thank you, too, for those who nurtured my spirit in other ways: those who read to me before I could read for myself; teachers who led the way to splendid insights and taught me skills that would see me through; Sunday school teachers and pastors whose words and deeds showed me how to live; and choir directors who encouraged me to sing praises to a personal God, from whom all blessings do surely flow.

Thank you, Lord, for all these things and many more, an abundance of blessings that have enriched the fabric of my life.

# ABOUT THE AUTHOR

**Terry C. Ley** was professor of English Education and Secondary Reading at Auburn University for twenty-seven years before his retirement in 2001. Before that, he taught middle school and high school English language arts for thirteen years in Iowa, where he grew up and earned degrees at the University of Northern Iowa and the University of Iowa. He was named a William T. Smith Distinguished Professor of Education at Auburn in 1998. Since retiring he has taught Writing Our Lives for the Osher Lifelong Learning Institute at Auburn for fifteen years and has provided literacy support for fourth graders at Wrights Mill Road School in Auburn, also for fifteen years.